The Religious Education We Need

The
Religious Education
We Need

TOWARD THE RENEWAL OF
CHRISTIAN EDUCATION

EDITED BY

James Michael Lee

CONTRIBUTORS

Alfred McBride
Randolph Crump Miller
Carl F. H. Henry
John Westerhoff III
Gloria Durka
James Michael Lee

Religious Education Press
Birmingham, Alabama

Printed in the United States of America

Library of Congress Catalog Card Number: 76-55587

ISBN: 0-89135-005-5

10 9 8 7 6 5 4 3
Religious Education Press
1531 Wellington Road
Birmingham, Alabama 35209

Religious Education Press Inc. publishes books and educational materials exclusively in religious education and in areas closely related to religious education. It is committed to enhancing and professionalizing religious education through the publication of significant scholarly and popular materials.

Contents

Introduction

One of the fundamental dimensions of religious education is its prophetic role. A prophet may or may not predict the future, but he always makes the future. A prophet is one who makes the future come more quickly than would be the case if he did not .exist. The work of God for which the prophet gives his life is that of ransoming the present with the coin of the future. To be a prophet is to hasten the future.

A Christian institution or a Christian movement, no less than an individual Christian, has an imperative to be prophetic. Such an imperative is burned into the soul of each Christian at baptism, and is given added urgency at confirmation. So too is the prophetic imperative infused into the mainstream of every institution and every movement which dares to call itself Christian.

Of all the sectors of the church's endeavor, few have so great a privilege and so great an obligation to be prophetic as religious education. Religious education by its nature pushes back the frontiers of an individual's or a culture's way of knowing, feeling, and living. Religious education is an activity by which the individual or society is helped to put on the new man, to be propelled more and more into actualizing the pleroma. If it is to fulfill its mission, religious education must not so much bring the now into the future as to bring the future into the now. This is true because the educational experience is not one of preparing the learner to live in the future but rather of helping the learner to live the future right now. To prepare for something in the future is always risky at best, for the future might never come, and when it does come, it often is not the kind of future we expected. It is more sensible to make the future come now, for then when the future does happen it will be that kind of future which we have made now.

The purpose of this book is avowedly prophetic, to hasten the future. It endeavors to jog our present complacency a bit, so that our conceptions and preconceptions can be rattled free enough that new configurations and procedures for religious education activity can thereby emerge. The past two decades were exciting times for religious education both in the new world and in the old. But now we are settling in, perhaps a bit too much. We do not seem to be making those bold leaps into the future and into the untried as much as we used to, and quite possibly religious education is in danger of becoming a bit calcified if not ossified as a result. This book is an attempt to shake up our present complacency in order that we will begin again, and in a much more fundamental way, to shape the future of religious education and through it the future of the Church and the world as well.

The aim of *The Religious Education We Need* is not to predict the future, or to indicate the kind of future we may expect to live in. Rather, the objective is to make the future, to offer visions and suggestions which will be enacted in the new, thereby making the future. The future belongs to those who make it, not to those who wait for it. A prophet does not simply hang around waiting for the future to come. A prophet is one who goes out with vision and vigor to make the future to be what it will be. A prophet is not so much one who walks into the future, but rather one who makes the future walk into the present.

To help attain the goal of *The Religious Education We Need*, I asked five distinguished religious educationists to join with me in giving their vision and perspective on what should be done to renew religious education. In extending the invitation to each of them to write a chapter, I asked only one thing: "Write what you want the future of religious education to be, and not what you think it will be." Thus this book is not a look into the crystal ball. It is not daydreaming, however pleasant daydreaming might be. Rather it is the presentation of visions, interpretations, policies, and practices which the various authors believe will make a better future for religious education.

The Religious Education We Need, then, is a prophetic endeavor. This volume hopes to play its part in shaping the future by offering ideas and proposals whereby the future can be effectively shaped. *The Religious Education We Need* is not a glimpse into the future, but rather a vision of what the future of religious education can and should be if we would but only make it that way.

No one Christian however learned, no one religious educationist however committed, no one Christian institution however hallowed enjoys a monopoly on the prophetic. Each Christian, each religious educationist, each Christian institution is called upon to be prophetic; each must be engaged in hastening the future, albeit from different vantage points. In our efforts to bring the future into the now, we would therefore be seriously remiss if we did not listen attentively to representatives of different backgrounds and perspectives, so that we might incorporate their own prophecy into our overall prophetic work. Thus, in this book I have attempted in my function as editor to provide the reader with prophetic statements by outstanding Christian religious educationists and educators of varying backgrounds, confessions, and stations. I have carefully surveyed the field, and was most fortunate to secure the collaboration of five outstanding colleagues who are generally acknowledged to be among the most eminent and most prophetic religious educationists in the United States. Three of the six contributors are Protestant, each representing a different yet complementary perspective. Randolph Crump Miller, widely recognized as the "dean of American Protestant religious educationists," is a priest of the Episcopal Church, editor of the field's most influential professional journal, *Religious Education,* and long-time professor of religious education at Yale University's Divinity School. John Westerhoff III, one of the most brilliant and captivating new stars in the religious education firmament, is an ordained minister in the United Church of Christ, and a professor of religious education in the divinity school at

Duke University. Carl F.H. Henry, known around the country as "Mr. Evangelical," is an ordained Baptist minister who for many years served as editor of Evangelical Protestantism's most influential and respected magazine, *Christianity Today,* and who currently is lecturer-at-large of World Vision International. Two other Roman Catholics have joined me in writing chapters. Alfred McBride, a priest of charm and distinction, is, in his post as director of the National Catholic Educational Association's National Forum of Religious Educators, as official a religious education representative of the institutional Catholic Church as one can possibly find. Gloria Durka, a young married woman who teaches religious education at Boston College, is one of the leading figures in the fresh and exciting new wave of Roman Catholic religious educationists who have emerged in recent years. I am providing these brief vignettes about the contributors to indicate the wide spectrum of prophecy and viewpoint encapsulated in this volume: Protestant and Catholic, Mainline Protestant and Evangelical Protestant, young and old, traditionalists and progressives, independents and representatives of official or semiofficial groups, administrators and professors, theologically-oriented and social-science oriented, Northern and Southern, men and women, and so forth.

A brief note on terminology might be in order. In the field, the term "religious education" is the one most commonly used, and the one which I believe is the most descriptive and the most accurate. Some Protestants, notably Evangelicals and Fundamentalists, prefer the designation "Christian education" because they contend that education cannot be religious unless it is Christian. Roman Catholics frequently employ the term "catechetics"; however, except for the "catechetical Establishment," this term is falling into deserved disuse because it is archaic, limited, and not adequately descriptive.

There is always a problem of cohesiveness in any volume in which there are many contributors. This is particularly true for books like this one, in which none of the contributors was given an assigned topic but instead was asked to write about what he or she would like religious education to become in the future. When I received all the chapters from my fellow-authors, I found to my delight that a definite pattern emerged. Thus I have arranged the chapters in a sequence in which I think they naturally flow. I put Alfred McBride's chapter in the lead-off position because it sets the whole tone and mood of the future, plunging the reader into the realm of that future which can be. McBride then goes on to sketch some important things which religious education must do, and do now, if it is to live fruitfully and Christianly in that future world which he has so engagingly and so compellingly drawn for us.

Randolph Crump Miller places religious education in its overarching historical perspective so that we can more readily appreciate where we have come from and, on this basis, gain some perspective on where, or where not, religious education should move. For Miller, religious education in the future must stress relationship—a Christian's relationship to God and to man—because Christianity is fundamentally a religion of relationships. Miller wishes to see future religious education focus on the facilitation of right relationship. Christian relationship should be promoted by a renewed attention to nurture and initiation; the activity generated by this renewed attention should proceed along the operating principles and practices of the discipline of education. Miller contends that any viable religious education for the future will have to consider the relationship of theology to religious education, and will have to begin to seriously stress the importance of pedagogical skills.

The middle two chapters of the book deal with two all-important and pivotal subject-matter contents of religious education, namely the bible and the liturgy. Carl Henry makes a strong case for the centrality of the bible in any future work of religious education. The bible is the living link between Christians of the future and Christians of the past, and indeed the living link between Christians of the future and Christ himself. Religious education in the future must work more vigorously than it has in the past to restore the whole world to Christ, and this task can only be accomplished, in the final analysis, by helping people attune their lives to the bible. Henry emphasizes that successful bible teaching just does not happen by chance—it must be carefully and deliberatively worked at. John Westerhoff regards the liturgy as the existential welding of a people into a religious community. People live their lives ritualistically, and so liturgy represents an outering and a communalizing of this pattern with the goal of making Christianity a living, relevant force in a person's life. The liturgy is, at bottom, religious education. The liturgy initiates people into that revolutionary community called Christianity. Religious education for the future should do more to fuse the ritual of worship with the ritual of a person's own developmental life, so that the whole of a person's existence will be a liturgy.

Setting the tone for the final two chapters of the book, Gloria Durka sees the main challenge of religious education's future as one of developing a whole new conception of religious education itself. As a starting point on the road to accomplishing this whole new conception, Durka suggests that we look at process itself—not just process at it is in the instructional process but also process as it is in the very goals of religious education. Goals are in process too, observes Durka. Process theology tries to inject process into the very heart of the reflective enterprise, so as to arrive at more dynamic and more living conceptualizations of God and of other religious realities. The centrality of process also suggests a whole new conception of professionalization in religious education, and also a reexamination of some of the power assumptions which have all too frequently hindered religious education from becoming what it should be.

In the last chapter of the book, I offer a concrete programmatic of what religious educators should do in the here-and-now if they wish to make their educational ministry truly prophetic. Professionalism is the key to an effective future for religious education. Professionalism implies that religious education be regarded as an autonomous area of work and not subservient to theology, that its practitioners be well-trained, and that it flow from fruitful theory. Operational guidelines which should undergird all religious education of the future include a fuller religionizing of religious education, a centering of the religious education enterprise in the family, a teaching ministry for Christians of every age and circumstance, and a radication of religious education in the overall work of the parish or congregation. Most of the last chapter provides concrete, eminently practical proposals for improving religious instruction, making the religion curriculum more effective, upgrading the training of religious educators, rendering administration more fecund, and helping religious guidance/counseling attain increased potency.

The Religious Education We Need is a highly practical and useful book. It gives each and every religious educator a wide variety of ideas by which he can go to work in his own ministry to better make that kind of future which religious education so urgently requires. Within the pages of this small volume there is a great wealth of suggestions on improving both the theory and the practice of religious education. But most of all, this book bodies forth a vision—a vision of five men and a woman who write on what they believe religious education should do if it is to truly ransom the present. Vision is all important, for without vision a people and its work will surely perish.

Speaking for myself, I have always regarded every Christian's basic purpose in life to be prophetic. I also believe that of all the church's endeavors, few have as great a potentiality to be truly and radically prophetic as religious education. It is the prophetic role of religious education which makes this apostolate so full of excitement but also so full of suffering. The prophet is at the outer edge of the whirlwind, a whirlwind he has often brought into being. But the whirlwind has its price, and its price is great and all-consuming. In the beginning, middle, and end, it is the prophet who must pay the great price. The others long since have run away and taken refuge in the mediocrity from whence they came. For some years now I have been engaged in reflection and research on a major work on the prophetic role of religious education. More years of preparation are needed before I undertake to write such a book. In the meantime, I hope this present little volume will serve to bring to some salience that prophetic function which should be at the nerve center of religious education.

The religious education which the future receives will be basically the religious education we forge today. We are called to be the prophets who will make the tomorrows, and if we fail in the prophetic vision and in the prophetic here-and-now practice, we will have failed the future. To fail the future is to fail ourselves, for the future is not only inhabited by people yet to be born, but also by ourselves who are destined to spend the rest of our lives in the future. To fail the future is to fail Christ, for Christ is the Omega, the process and the end-point of all time beyond the present time.

Notre Dame, Indiana   JAMES MICHAEL LEE
April 28, 1976

CHAPTER I

The Stuff of Dreams

Alfred McBride

Like most people I am interested in the future, if for no other reason than I plan to spend all of my life there. If the past is prologue to all that will happen in the future, so also is the immediate past out of which I do my thinking and planning. I am of the conviction that conscious human effort can do something to shape the future, even though such energy is an unwilling co-partner with impersonal and sometimes fatalistic forces that frustrate the "best laid plans of mice and men."

One way to exert a vital influence upon the shape of the future is to construct a desirable scenario. Wishing may not make it so, but the wish is father to the thought and millions have testified that their dreams do come true. Da Vinci dreamed of airplanes and Jules Verne of submarines. The realists laughed and the cynics scorned. But here we are flying at supersonic speeds and sailing under a polar ice cap.

Utopias and Erewhons are a necessary counterpoint to mechanical and mathematical projections. Let Delphi technicians assert their probability curves. I will take the other route of an equally honorable tradition, namely, what some people call pipe dreaming and others a passionate vision. I intend to spin out a vision of Catholic education as I would desire to see it take shape within the reasonable future. How many years from now? 1984? A little too soon, though I hope my musings would help avert any Orwellian takeover of Catholic education.

How about the year 2000, that favorite of think tank millenialists? Maybe that is too far away. Generations used to occur in 25 to 50 year spans. Now one breaktaking decade may be a generation and a half. Still, I'll settle for my dream coming true somewhere near the year 2000.

My work and my life have been situated in Catholic education, and it is primarily from this perspective and to this task that this chapter will deal.

I will use the expression Catholic education in its broader sense, hence including Catholic schools, colleges, and universities, as well as religious education centers with concomitant approaches to families and adults. I write as one working in the National Catholic Educational Association, an organization that for the first 60 years of its existence concerned itself mainly with Catholic schools, but which in recent years has expanded its services to every form of religious education.

Both as a long-time Catholic high school teacher and Catholic university professor and as now a staff member of the NCEA, I will naturally possess the kind of bias that years of association with school-oriented education gives me. I hope, however, that this is a background that will help me to speak meaningfully to the broader range of Catholic education. Happily, other authors in this book will put some insight into any blind spots which may afflict me.

I will use the style of scenario writing to express what I want to see occur in Catholic education in the future. In letting my imagination take over I am not pondering the likelihood of the following ideas, but rather affirming that this is what I wish to happen. Hence this essay is more than crystal ball gazing. It is an attempt to express my wishes about the future in a dramatic story format. I call it the stuff of dreams. I want it to be a reality.

The remainder of this chapter will embody my dream, a dream I hope will become a reality.

MY WISH FOR THE FUTURE

What kind of Catholic education would I like to see circa 2000? I see Catholic schools and religious education centers thriving. Fifty percent of all Catholic parishes have schools. The remaining 50% have centers. Ninety percent of all young people, ages 7–18, are involved in regular, systematic religious education. No youth education occurs apart from family education.

The majority of Catholic adults of 2000 have accepted as part of their religious commitment a lifelong dedication to personal religious maturing, which will involve education as a component. The result is that more Catholic adults will be involved in adult forms of religious learning than youth. This is not because the youth are being progressively ignored (90% of them are engaged) but simply because, if the demographers are right, there will be more adults.

A Full Support System

The church of 2000 is a real support system for Catholic education. Not just moral and economic support—but also ideological. The gap between church leadership policy and ideology, so lamentably broad in the Dark Ages of the 70's, has disappeared. Educators in 2000 are not lapsing into embarrassing double talk and fainthearted apology (let alone plain silence) on moral and belief issues that marked the chaotic late 60's and early 70's.

There is a united front between the *text* (schools and centers) and the *context* (church community and leadership). This united front is not a mindless uniformity. Pluralism on belief and value issues is now a reality. Not a pluralism without parameters. That would be sheer relativity.

The fundamental realities of revelation (creation, incarnation, redemption, sacraments, future life) are heard of in a wide variety of languages. Principles of moral valuing are brought to bear upon an immensely new expanse of moral dilemmas that include the proposal to clone recruits for the government's armed forces and a pill that relieves the discomforts of nightly orgiastic dining.

Disco-vision Revolution

Seventy-five percent of all students (schools, centers, adults) in the year 2000 are learning input exclusively from disco-vision. The remaining ones are still committed to the primacy of book learning, though many of their "books" are basically printouts that issue them information on demand from a world library data information bank. It is clear that the leadership of the Catholic community is coming from the TV trained students, while the more philosophical-counseling types graduate from the Book People centers.

As disco-vision moved to the center of the learning experience, books and written materials became the auxiliary props. People now speak of mediaographies rather than bibliographies. As might be expected, this revolution in method spawned much disturbance in the world of teachers. Angry parades, sitouts and other perennial forms of protest preceded capitulation. Hot speeches about intellectual disaster, the media as narcotic and other similar ploys failed to stem the tide.

The arrival of a home disco-vision turntable—now as common as the audio turntable—along with movie-sized screens solved many problems that plagued teachers for years. For one thing it guaranteed that the so-called "affective domain" so much desired during the Book Age, but often so difficult to achieve, is now a normal component of the learning process. The very vividness of TV input assured that.

It has also brought to an unheard of realization the possibility of the tutorial as the normative method of instruction. The teacher, freed from the tediousness of preparation (i.e., becoming living books), lets TV's living book take care of that demand. Instead, the teacher now has the time to devote to personal engagement with each student, thus recapturing the ancient meaning of *magister* namely master/mistress and disciple.

The first ones to see the value of this method of educating were the personnel of the religious education centers. The TV home delivery system, the convenience, economy, and variety offered by the discs, suddenly brought a "master teacher" into every corner of every parish. Adults and youth could begin with the same input. The differential was in the output, as different levels of maturity interacted and family learning quantum leaped.

Many who feared that the power of logic, concept, and thought would be destroyed by preoccupation with *emotional* pictures found that the intellect flourished as it had not done since the Renaissance. Those who thought that religion and faith would suffer found themselves enjoying a religious revival that American historical culturalists compared favorably to the "Great Awakening" of Jonathan Edwards.

Far from making the mind a desert, the juices of media-produced affectivity, expanded the power of wonder in the human mind and brought into favorable prominence the writings of Plato, Augustine, Bonaventure, and Duns Scotus. Their holistic intellectual approach moved contemporary philosophy and theology beyond the subjectivism of mid-20th century personalism to the desired dream of intersubjectivity hoped for by men such as Buber and Marcel.

The emphasis in religion in the year 2000 has moved to the mystical and transcendental, quite similar to the ideational periods described by Pitirim Sorokin in his analysis of culture in his *Crisis of Our Age*. Practical altruism and justice-seeking are not missing. In fact, they are rampant, but, oddly enough, the rhetoric and asceticism that brings this about effectively evinces a mystical mood that has surprisingly practical results.

The Goal: Spiritual Enlightenment

Goals of spiritual enlightenment in the year 2000 are freely discussed and agreed on as desirable aims of Catholic education. Many teachers, not just the religion ones, spend summers in Trappist and Carmelite monasteries and Indian ashrams. Interestingly, the American cloisters usually have a team of *humanist* therapists integrated into the community to create a coalition between mind altering experimental research along with the results that come from classical contemplative disciplines.

One happy result of placing spiritual enlightenment as a primary goal of Catholic education is that the mysteries of dogma have been liberated from narrowly intellectual truth claims (though they remain as such) into windows through which the transcendent may be perceived. Dogma thus becomes a mysterious pointer to the beyond in our midst, causing sentiments of radical amazement and the shock of recognition of God's presence in the affairs of people. This enlarging of the role of truth claims has made them immensely relevant in the religious maturing of the Catholic students (including the adult students).

It has also affected positively the appreciation of moral principles. The processes of moral valuing, rather than being mod versions of a narrowly intellectualist casuist approach, indicate the intrinsic connection between the lived experience of God in spiritual enlightenment, and the inner radical demand to move outward to create a moral and just society. One result of this is the widespread popularity of the life and writings of Gandhi.

The emphasis on spiritual enlightenment has restored the role of the fast and sexual continence in the context of the church and the text of its educational mission. No longer a law of the church, but now more intensely practiced than when it was, such voluntary spiritual discipline has gained an impressive following. For ecumenical reasons, many Catholics practice the fast of Ramadan with Moslems for the eventual unity of the two religions, as well as for the intrinsic merit of the act itself.

I mentioned earlier that by the year 2000 many teachers are going on extended monastic retreats. A new movement among college students, following the ancient custom of Buddhist youth in Thailand, is the so-called mininovitiate. They are asking a temporary three month admission to the novitiates of religious orders as a final preparation for their spiritual adventure in the world.

Needless to say, this movement not only has increased the membership of such orders, but also bred a corps of spiritual leaders for society. Like any development, the emphasis on spiritual enlightenment met with its own opposition in Catholic education. Many parishioners and parents balked when, in some cases, a Buddhist monk or Hindu guru was hired for the meditation training programs. The people were offended by even the thought of bringing such "pagans" into a school or parish center. They were temporarily mollified when the pope issued an encyclical about the value of the meditative techniques of Buddhism and Hinduism.

Ecumenism

Which brings me to the subject of ecumenism and its contextual effect on Catholic education in the year 2000. Much to the joy of everyone (well, almost), the dialogues both between Catholics and Anglicans, and also between Catholics and Lutherans, resulted in their emergence as sister churches within the universal Catholic church community. They hold a status similar to the one formerly enjoyed by the so-called Eastern rite "uniate" churches.

By the year 2000 the uniates as such have disappeared since practically the entire Orthodox church has come into communion with Rome. Canterbury, "Augsburg," and Constantinople are now a part of the one, catholic, holy, and apostolic church, acknowledging the pope as chief ecumenical bishop and sign of authority for the majority of the world's Christians. The TV church history discs now treat the Great Schism and the Reformation substantially as a relic of the past.

Of course there is still the problem of the remaining Protestant communions. One interesting sign is that the World Council of Churches has moved its headquarters to Rome. Serious dialogue with Baptists, Methodists, Presbyterians, and other Evangelical churches is in full swing. Needless to say, the *disaffection* of the Anglicans and Lutherans has shaken fellow Protestants. But the one world consciousness effected by the media, transportation, and the once cursed multinational corporations has done much to lay the cultural groundwork for the unity of all Christians.

The results of the negotiations with Orthodoxy, Anglicans, and Lutherans did not deprive the pope of some measure of ruling power. The initial guidelines drawn up seem to have worked very well. What is more we have been blessed with a pope whose credibility with the world stands high. He has the capacity to absorb and reflect an immense variety of expressions. He has strengthened the committees working with Buddhists, Hindus, and Moslems.

The arrival of Episcopalians and Lutherans as sister churches has caused many administrative flurries in America. Who is in charge of whom? What about sacraments, especially eucharist and marriage? How does it affect the territorial parishes? These are currently being worked out. Guidelines are piling up on everyone's desks, especially the pastors, the religious education coordinators, and the principals. As usual, the ones seemingly least concerned are the students whose youthful openness welcomes this development.

Many Episcopalians and Lutherans feared their people would not go along with the change. Some did not. Most have. And in fact the change seems to have infused new vitality into our sister churches, as well as in our own.

National Catechetical Directory

One thing that seemed to help everyone accept the changes was the fallout from the success of the process used by the National Catechetical Directory (NCD) back in the 70's. It was the greatest consultation in the history of the Catholic church up to that time. Not only was the consultation phenomenal, its result was nothing less than visionary in its impact.

It put in motion things we take for granted now in the year 2000: the prevalence of adult education, the maturity of religious education centers, the stable witness of value-centered Catholic schools, the acceptance of the behavioral sciences as legitimate and helpful copartners in religious education, the equal rights financing for religious education centers, the pastoral tone of diocesan offices. All these were contained in the vision of the NCD. Today they are so obvious, one wonders that they were ever a problem.

Liturgy

Which leads me to the subject of liturgy, with which catechesis must always be concerned. Perhaps never in history have our people been so aware of the value of ritual and celebration as they are now in the year 2000. I think much of this is due to the revolution in education caused by TV as well as to the shift toward spiritual enlightenment.

As I mentioned earlier, we have come to see in practice an intellectual approach constantly fed by the affective dimension. In the year 2000, we no longer speak of liturgy of Word as distinct from liturgy of Sacrament. We do not see the first part of liturgy as sort of the mind set for the second half which is ritual set. The whole experience is a ritual. Our songs and chants (and mantras too) at the beginning have a stately hieratic quality to them. Our declaration of the scriptural word is clearly proclaimed in a ritual manner. It is read, and very well read. Seminary training emphasizes the dignity and power of the well read Word.

I do not want to leave the wrong impression. We are by no means puppets nervously going through prescribed motions. One example, which I am afraid is not too helpful to you, is that of the Japanese Kabuki dramatic tradition. It is highly stylized and yet intensely human. It adheres to form without becoming death-dealing and suffocating formalism.

We are partly saved by the varieties of the liturgical year itself with its progress of high feast and ordinary times. We are also liberated by a marvelous diversity of forms at our disposal. Further we are aided by an extensive training of our celebrants in the "body talk" of ritual behavior. Gestures and movements are not seen as blind instructions, but "forms of speech" that possess a transparency, pointing to and revealing the divine presence at worship.

This is why spiritual enlightenment has been such an invaluable support for our liturgical development. We are increasingly blessed with celebrants who come to us with a strong sense of inwardness. When their very gestures communicate a mood of depth and the beyond, we do not have much fear that liturgy, so well prepared for by our religion teachers, will disappoint those being prepared.

Clergy Sabbaticals

One thing that has made a difference is that in the year 2000 all American dioceses mandate a one-year sabbatical every ten years for parish clergy, in addition to a one-week renewal each year. We have well over 35 such sabbatical centers right now. They emphasize a total communal experience with components of spiritual enlightenment, intellectual development (in the holistic sense), deepening of ritual capability, along with pragmatic data about parish life, a strengthening of media consciousness, and the arts of communal exchange.

Yes, there are still sermons at liturgy. However, the pastor usually preaches only once a month. Other people in the parish are called upon to deliver homiletic reflections and spiritual testimonies. Occasionally we are treated to a video-homily. This is always the case for the annual pastoral "letter" of the bishop.

Are sermons better than they used to be? Infinitely. A survey conducted in 1999 showed that 92% of all parishioners were pleased with the preaching. Many pastors subscribe to a video-homily service which seems to be an enormously helpful self-starter for most of them. At the same time I must caution you to recall that the ritualistic mood so characterizes our liturgy reshapes the homily from being a wordy and preachy time-out-for-words to a rhythm that is more characteristic of ritual itself. At the risk of being misunderstood, I would say today's sermons reflect an oracular stance. Not oracle in the sense of prediction, but in the biblical meaning of prophetic utterance—thus says the Lord.

Since liturgy has evolved in the manner I have described, it is far easier for us to have a religious education that can honestly say it is preparing people for a liturgy that is really there. All liturgical celebrants spend time with our students, initiating them into their own insights and approach to ritual. Every religious instruction program reviews discs that cover a wide variety of the world's revered rituals in all belief systems. The reverence and awe that comes through in these experiences has a valued effect upon our students.

One cultural development that began back in the 70's has produced a more than favorable appreciation of ritual, and that is the popular love affair with classical dancing. The phenomenal growth of ballet and other forms of interpretative dancing has trained a generation of people how to read the meaning of movement in so stylized a format. The sacred dance is now a regular part of our liturgy, especially on high holy days. It is hard to remember that this was once so rare.

The sacramental preparation of students in the year 2000 is always a full-blown family event. Our skills at individualization so developed that each student is taken when they clearly seem to be ready for an initiation into a new sacrament. We have many advanced and refined ways to ascertain the personal level and receptivity of each student.

Cold as it may sound, an extensive printout on each student is kept. The national parish transfer-data-system makes possible an instant recall system on information about each student, and parishioner as well, so that our high rate of mobility (35% of Americans in the year 2000 move every year) does not affect service to parishioners adversely. Yes, we worried about this becoming an ecclesiastical Big Brother.

So far so good. Extensive safeguards of each person's confidentiality and right of privacy are structured in. From what I can see, there has not been much abuse of this. The data is considered sacred and subject to the protection of what we used to call "the seal." My experience has been so favorable in this matter that I think I can predict with confidence that no major abuse is likely to happen.

Media Evangelization

The current dialogue with the Baptists which began in 1996 is causing a ripple of demand in our church to make infant baptism optional. Predictably, some of the more liberal parishes are pushing to experiment with this. Should this come about, then the current forms of sacramental preparation will undergo revision upwards toward adulthood. We already have a model in the baptismal religious instruction program during Lent. Incidentally, that has exploded in recent years with an amazing number of converts from 90 million so-called unchurched in our nation. I think some of that is due to the success of the remarkably tasteful commercials from the coalition of the Franciscan and Paulist communication centers, who now function as subsidiaries for the National Catholic Television Network.

I must admit I still feel a bit uneasy at seeing such a pitch in the middle of a soap opera (yes, in the year 2000 we still have them) or a Super Bowl, but the clear soft sell and lack of patronizing seems to touch the viewers the right way. Another element you may not be able to appreciate is that our unchurched are really that way. Millions of them have never had any contact with mainline religion, so when they finally come in contact with it, they are really hearing news—and good news, at that.

Still, there is another way that many of our unchurched, and the churched as well, receive an unexpected lesson in the meaning of religion. And that is the movies. Gone completely are the movie palaces of old, although their asphalt counterparts, the outdoor movie, do remain. The small movie lounges, so popularized in the 70's, are to be found everywhere.

Why do people still leave their movie-sized TV sets and super-market-priced discs? The movie theaters in the year 2000 provide three dimensional films with a technology not yet adapted to home use. The process is called holography. However, what is more important for our topic here is that major film producers regularly make genuinely religious films.

Much of this began in the early 1980's when the Vatican financed the filming of Luke's gospel and asked Fellini to be the director. Probably not since Pope Julius commissioned Michelangelo to decorate the Sistine Chapel had the Holy See placed so deep an investment in a contemporary art form. The result was stunning. Fellini, the anticlerical chronicler of religious foibles, produced a religious masterpiece that turned the screen into a contemporary form of a Renaissance canvas. Both a commercial and artistic success, it was also a religious event that portrayed a Jesus who could speak to and heal a modern world.

Once this ice was broken, other major film makers put their hand to religious themes and questions as major personal efforts. As in anything, some succeeded and some failed. Most importantly, the precedent was established and spiritual questions were raised for millions who might never darken the door of a church. By now, as you can well imagine, most of the productions of the 80's and 90's are on discs and part of our local libraries.

Schools and Centers

I want to switch gears at this point and tell you about what our schools and centers in the year 2000 are like. America today has 30,000 Catholic parishes. I am not including the Episcopalian and Lutheran ones, since we have no accurate data yet. Fifteen thousand of our parishes have schools. The average school enrolls 300 students. Half of all the teachers are religious and the other half are laity.

Religious are on equal salary with the laity and no special benefits accrue to the religious. Everyone is treated alike. It looked for a while as though the religious were about to abandon schools as an apostolate. Just as everyone had taken this for a fact, there was a turnaround. The traditional orders reaffirmed their commitment to Catholic education—both schools and centers. A dozen new American based orders emerged choosing Catholic education as their principal apostolate.

While many schools in the year 2000 have a mix of laity and religious, over 7,000 are conducted by laymen. In the schools where there is a mixture, the leadership roles go to the best qualified. The salaries for all Catholic school personnel are competitive with their counterparts in public education. Parishes with schools universally budget for the full religious education of all Catholic youth in the parish. In most cases this means a team of no less than three fully salaried religious educators plus finances for all hard- and software required. All Catholic educators, both for school and center, are considered as one total educational community dedicated to the full educational needs of the parish.

The remaining 15,000 parishes have religious education centers, all with fully budgeted personnel and facilities to do the work needed to help every member of the parish in their religious educational development. Again, like the schools, around half of all the personnel are religious and the other half are laity. Salaries are generous and competitive and social benefits mandatory.

Noise-Free Environment

The movements I have mentioned above have had a profound effect on the shape of education in these schools and centers. The dominance of disco-vision has totally eliminated the school desk as the main image. Seminar rooms, learning lounges, resource centers, privacy pods, instant printouts, tape deck viewing and listening areas, as well as a small auditorium (not a school hall) give you some idea of what our schools and centers look like.

What do they sound like?

They are quiet. But then so is much of our society in the year 2000. I am happy to report that the old campaign against noise pollution won. Actually a new industry has grown up to create a society that can enjoy a noise-free existence. Schools are quiet not because of rules but because machines, acoustical fabrics, and materials have been wondrously silenced. In fact, things are so quiet that industry sometimes introduces what they call "white noise." This is simply a deliberate addition of some murmur or purr to reassure some people that the machines are really working. Engineers have done wonders with auto engines and plane motors. Believe it or not, we enjoy a silence that is velvet. The major noise now is of human origin. The peace of the technological milieu has taken the nervous sting out of the raucousness of human noise.

Fear not, however, the noise level at sports and parties is suitably loud. People do still get headaches, though not as often. The tranquilizer industry has just about gone out of business, except for use in hospitalization. The learning environment today seems to echo Merton's description of a sun-drenched Cistercian cloister in southern France toward the end of the misnamed Dark Ages.

When the noise is simply the chatter of people engaged in the process of learning, there is not the mechanistic Babel that has cursed so much of learning during the ponderous Gutenberg period. Thus the noise that once polluted our environment, and was actually a perverse reassurance to mechanical/technological man that these machines really were important (who said they weren't?). I am proud to say we have progressed beyond the brute demand for a noisy yea-saying from our creatures. We know they are there, and we want them now to keep quiet. We insist that the only noises made be those of a meaning that ministers to the expansion of our inwardness.

Neo-Tutorial Instruction

Are our schools and centers in the year 2000 faithful to the typical hopes of professional educators, say in the areas of curriculum planning, teacher competency, and evaluation? In other words, are they logical, systematic, capable of long range thinking and investment?

Yes and no.

Yes, they are perfectly capable of thought, even metaphysical, if you wish, in spite of all the affective juices I mentioned earlier in this chapter. Yet I think you would be unsettled by our approach because you basically have no existing model similar to ours. Perhaps Oxford University would be the one place, though medieval/Victorian in format, that most closely approximates what we are about. Probably also certain small but highly expensive academies come close to an image of our educational way of life.

The difference with us is that we have made the aristocratic model available to all our students. Just as everyone who has arrived at Oxford or the posh academies is not the brightest of students, so neither are ours. But like those old venerable institutions we can realize their potential through our coalition with technology to effect the space-age tutorial in a manner undreamed of by modular schedulers and individualized instructors. The sheer flexibility of our technology makes the wildest flexibilities of our imaginations possible and down to earth.

Limits of Logic

This is why the terms *systematic* and *development along curricular design paths* must be reunderstood. The same with logic. Before I go any further, I think we must face the fact that such illusions as logic, system, and development were always precisely that, fabrications of the mind that seldom found realization in individual people's lives.

Logic, system, and development, when set as the backdrop for educating people and ruthlessly applied, would make either teacher or student into a madman/woman. That is why they were so seldom taken seriously. They partake of a myth no less unreal than the so-called myths which vocational conceptualists spurned as naive representations of the really real.

In their heart of hearts people have always known the fatal weakness of logical constructs, namely, that real life is too oceanic to contain so frail a guideline. I think the beauty and honesty of our world is that we recognize this and really do treat a construct as just that and nothing more. The result is that we often talk more about metalogic in our educational planning system than of what we consider to be a one dimensional logic and system which we read about in the instructional and planning manuals of an earlier age.

Yes, we know how to do chain reasoning. We know about beginnings, middles, and ends. We appreciate goals and accountability. I think the difference with us is that we are overly conscious of the limitations therein involved, and we are equipped financially, personally and mechanically to deal with reality with unimaginable flexibility, by your standards, in the processes of education.

Which brings me to the matter of the nonrational in educational planning. Educators of the 60's indulged in nonrational fantasies.

The results were as chaotic as the plans, naturally. The point seemed to be that gut sharing might be the sum and substance of what education was all about. Typically, this was an overreaction to rationalist views of education.

I blush to recall how many religion classes found such a love affair with irrational or nonrational man so exciting and meaningful. Meaningful? How could it be when powers of reflection that would arrive at meaning were seldom tapped. Instead feeling was called meaning, and a barbaric darkness settled over many. Small wonder. Essays on nonrational man are not supposed to deny rational man.

Even that redoubtable intellectualist Aristotle clearly speaks of the legitimate and necessary tension that will and must always exist between the rational and nonrational in humans. I am pleased, though not overweening I trust, to assert that we retain a healthy consciousness of the tension between the rational and nonrational dimensions of life and education. Odd as it may seem, we do indeed exult in the powers of reason, but we are also highly sensitized to the world of intuition, emotion, and the mystery of what Heidegger calls the prerational or prereflexive.

I think that the way in which our culture has developed has helped us to live in that realm of light caused by the sparking interaction of reason with the nonreason aspects within us. The relationship is not a grudging truce in the face of tension, but rather a purposeful collaboration of the wild horses that would each want to go its own way. We will not let them. And we are the richer for that.

CONCLUSION

In sum, what then do I want to see for Catholic education for the year 2000? It is a world in which the method has radically changed due to TV technology and the victory of the antinoise polluters. It is a culture that favors the goal of spiritual enlightenment as the primary aspiration of education, an aim so well suited to Catholic schools and centers.

It is a time when ecumenism has largely succeeded, the leadership of the pope assumed a new shape and overtures to other great world religions is beginning to be taken seriously. It is an era when both Catholic schools and religious education centers flourish. It is an epoch that sees the rejuvenation of the religious orders and a continuing growth of the participation of the laity in every level of church decision making.

It is a milieu wherein the dream of philosophers as diverse as Aristotle and Kant achieves realization in the educators' acceptance of the ancient and productive tension between the rational and the nonrational. It is all this and much more, since no reality can ever be embraced by the words that try to express it. Poets indeed agonize, and do occasionally arrive at a word event, that comes close to saying it all. Still, onward we try to say it in ever new ways.

I have presented here a dream, a Utopia, an Erewhon that I wish to see in the future of Catholic education. I have not tried to give a picture of everything I want for the year 2000. I didn't say too much about adult and family education. I obviously dwelt more on context than text, because I have come to know how central the context is to what the text would like to do. I have puzzled enough about context to know that. Hence my long digressions on religious and cultural context in the year 2000.

I once heard from a friend that biblical prophets were so great because they thought wildly about God and people. I cannot hope to be a certified member of that remarkable fraternity, but there is nothing to stop me from thinking as wildly as I wish, especially when I am so invited by the editor of this book. On my own terms, I think I have done just that.

I will be gratified to know not that you agreed with me (nor annoyed that you disagreed), but rather that I might have given you a momentary—or prolonged—sense of freedom to go off and do your own fantasizing about your own desires for the future. I am sure that religious education will not suffer from your cloudy excursions. In fact I will wager that we will all be so much the better for it.

Yes, lest I have in any way led you into an overserious aspect, I conclude with Shakespeare's thoughts about the stuff of dreams:

Be cheerful, sir,
Our revels are now ended. These our actors,
As I foretold you, were all spirits, and
Are melted into air, into thin air:
And, like the baseless fabric of this vision,
The cloud-capped towers, the gorgeous palaces,
The solemn temples, the great globe itself,
Yea, all which it inherit, shall dissolve,
And, like this insubstantial pageant faded,
Leave not a rack behind. We are such stuff
As dreams are made on; and our little life
Is rounded with a sleep.
                    The Tempest, Act 4, Scene 1

CHAPTER II

Continuity and Contrast in the Future of Religious Education

Randolph Crump Miller

A vision of what I would like to see in the field of religious education would have to include much that is occurring in the present, a recovery of some important insights from the past, and an adventure in creative emergents as we form the future. My perspective is that of a practitioner who has been involved in the creation of the theory of practice, who has worked on curriculum development, and who has been in charge of education in the parish. My concern in this chapter will be education in the parish or synagogue, and only indirectly in a school, college, or university.

PAST AND PRESENT

My first exposure to religious education was during the declining years of the Religious Education Movement in the 1930's, when the giants were George Albert Coe, George Herbert Betts, William Clayton Bower, Adelaide Case, Paul Herman Vieth, and Luther Allen Weigle. The influence of these people was tremendous, especially in the International Council of Religious Education (formed in 1922), but it was overcome by the onslaught of neo-orthodoxy, and only in the 1950's did it reoccur with a new theological slant, which might be called existentialism.

The modern period in Protestantism began in the 1950's with developments in the Episcopal Church. The emphasis was on relationships, with a debt to Martin Buber and Reuel Howe. The questions centered on "Who am I?" "Who are you?" "Where are we going?" The Christian faith was understood as providing answers to these questions through faith in God who acts, revealed in the scriptures. Methodologically, it was based on creative teaching, reliance on parental influences, and worship as a central factor. The Christian heritage was to be used as an accumulated wisdom that would open pupils to the current activity of God in and through human relationships, and salvation was conceived as a psycho-physical wholeness that was based on trust in God. The impact of this development was strong in the minority of parishes that took it seriously, but there was resistance from those who either were caught up on the older liberal theology or those who were still relying on the old content-centered method backed by conservative biblical theology. There was considerable spinoff as other denominations modified this approach so as to avoid the risks of the users of the Episcopal Seabury Series. The United Church of Christ was influenced by this approach, and later the Anglican Church of Canada made full use of the Seabury educational theory and resources for their own materials.

Catholicism had its own revolution, sparked by Vatican II and centered on a rediscovery of the bible. The catechism was relegated to the teachers as a propositional summary and the emphasis was on kerygma. The telling of the biblical story as a means for helping the student relate to God was consistent with some of the insights of the Seabury Series. The language for such teaching avoided propositional forms and sought to communicate in what came to be called "poetic simple." There was some modification of this approach, and soon there were many resource materials, especially audio-visuals, that were used by Protestants and Catholics.

Somewhere near the end of the 1960's, there was what I would call a failure of nerve among Protestant educational bureaucrats. As they saw their budgets being cut, sales of their expensive resources declining, and interest in education at a low ebb, leadership at the national level was restricted. There were exceptions to this, and enthusiasm in the Lutheran Church of America remained high. Catholic commitment and morale improved, even with the shift in policy from parochial schools to the local parish as the domain of much education. One reason for the shift among Protestants was fewer students, due partially to the lower birth rate. The high enthusiasm and the demands on teachers and congregations in the 1950's drew on the energies of the congregations and soon these energies were depleted and many parishes settled for a second-best (or lower) policy of education. Partly, also, lower morale was due to failure to fulfill the high hopes held by those who had engineered and introduced the resources in that period, for it never became clear that resources contain no magic and that the successful use of them depends on people and on the quality of life in the congregation. Furthermore, education was in competition for its finances with the militant champions of social action. Concern about race, poverty, minority, and civil rights became high priority items, and properly so, but because of the conservative nature of most parishes this led to smaller budgets for all operations, including social action.

At this point, a few social scientists who were watching the downward trend in morale and attendance predicted that within a few years there would be no Sunday schools. Some parents seemed to share this conclusion and made it a self-fulfilling prophecy by withdrawing or not even enrolling their children. But others responded by indicating that although they had been deserted at the high bureaucratic level there was much that could be done at the grass roots. New developments, often creative and imaginative, began at the parish level. It was a local option approach, finding help wherever it existed, selecting resources wherever they could be found, and often ignoring the official materials of their own denomination. Often these materials were those developed by Roman Catholics and used in Protestant Sunday schools, or developed by Protestants and Jews and used in Roman Catholic CCD classes and parochial schools. This cross-fertilization has rich possibilities.

It is hard to characterize the grass-roots developments. They are diverse. Some are attempts by incompetent but concerned clergy and lay people, who use the cheapest of commercially-prepared materials or develop their own. What they have going for them is enthusiasm, and this enlists the loyalty of the pupils and parents even when the content would make any biblical scholar or theologian shudder. Others are imaginative programs based on the way people learn, geared to their interests and capacities, and based on the best of modern theological thinking and pedagogical procedures.

Experiments have been tried. They are not panaceas, but they offer a degree of novelty and a variety of approach that justifies them for a place in an overall program. One of the most important, especially for an educational center with an inadequate number of rooms, is the open classroom. Some would argue that this is *the* solution, but others would say that it belongs in the rhythm of learning as one option, to be used from time to time. It puts demands on teachers for both flexibility and expertness, but it may just fit in with some teachers' aptitudes for that program only. Especially when it is a part of an overall policy of short term units it has possibilities. The short term approach, for example of ten weeks, focuses on a problem, or question, or content for a limited period of time, with a teacher who is committed for that period only. There may be a mixture of formal and informal classes, of a variety of topics, of graded or ungraded groups depending on interest. Ungraded classes, however, may also be used in the open classroom or in formal classrooms without the short term approach. The idea of the ungraded class may lead to the concept of family clusters, with several families meeting together as a regular educational activity, replacing or supplementing the other procedures.

These experimental approaches suggest that unless there is a body of informed adults, nothing much of importance will occur. We need adult education to train teachers and to incorporate parents in the education of children. So far, such programs seem to be lagging. But we need adult education for reasons that are not simply expedient. When we recall that many adults stopped their religious education between the ages of ten and sixteen and that

Christianity is primarily a faith of adults, we see how much adults are short-changed when we think of education for children only. Education should be from womb to tomb, with special emphasis on the education of mature adults so that they will have some understanding of what has been called the priesthood or the ministry of the laity.

One other recent development needs to be noted: the discovery of the organic relationship between worship and education. This became clear to me in the parish I grew up in, in a parish I was minister to, and in the experiments of Ernest Ligon. In the latter two situations, the goal was worship for parents and children together, along with other adults, geared so that the children knew they belonged. The practice of worship for families-as-a-unit has developed in many ways, some of them unsatisfactory (especially when the clergyman insists on a sermon for adults only, ignoring the children's level of understanding, or when it becomes what is called a "squirmers' Mass"), but when it works it becomes a part of the total educational experience. In many denominations children are now included as recipients of the elements at Communion services, music that appeals to the younger generation is sung, and preaching can be based on images that are concrete enough for children to respond to them. After the service, parents and adults have classes when the children do. Some parishes now organize their Sunday morning program in this way, ending with a celebration based on what has happened in the earlier worship and the class periods.

Where these developments have been successful, there have been important by-products which are essential to sound education. The chief by-product is the sense of community. I am not sure that this can be programmed, although there have been good results over a short period of time in certain kinds of group process. Such procedures may issue in a small nucleus within a congregation that can stimulate the development of the sense of community, or can lead to a clique within a congregation and destroy whatever sense of community is there. The sense of community is the way in which people satisfy their urge to belong, to be human in relation to other human beings; it is important to both children and adults.

THE FUTURE

Community

As we look to the future, we need to draw on those developments of the past and present that are worthwhile. One place to start is by an examination of community. There is a quality of relationships that provides the meaning of a community. We see what is meant by quality when we examine the nature of the family in which children and parents and sometime grandparents are nurtured. There is a language of relationships that communicates love, trust, committed concern for others, reconciliation, or lack of love, mistrust, indifference, and alienation. There is sometimes a pendulum-like swing from one set of qualities to another, and unless there is a possibility of understanding and forgiveness the community itself may dissolve. Families move in both directions, and our key to understanding and predicting what may happen is based on our sensing the quality of the relationships. Often the key to whether the relationships are sound lies with the controlling person or persons. Children become helpless in the face of parental discord, but a strong parent can often set up relationships by which children's alienations and conflicts can be healed within the dynamics of creative meaning.

A school depends on its quality of relationships for its sense of community, which becomes the precondition of sound learning. We speak of the morale of a school, and when it is destroyed by inept administration, teaching, or personal relations the level of learning goes down. It would oversimplify things to claim that a good school principal makes *all* the difference, for there are complex factors in the neighborhood that cannot be controlled from within the school; but a poor principal can destroy morale even when other factors are positive. If we are to straighten out our views of education in terms of quality of life within the school community, we need research into the factors needed for healthy community and those which tend to destroy it.

What we have said about family and school applies also to a congregation and its educational activities. Much that is attempted by competent teachers and interested students can be compromised by a low quality of congregational life. Like parents in the family and principals in schools, the pastor is a key person. The educational program in a parish is often a reflection of the pastor's dedication, insight, and ability, and also of the quality of life that one's ministry engenders. Negatively, it can be said that the pastor is the chief bottleneck, and positively that he or she is the source of inspiration for a sound educational program. There are many other factors that need to be looked at, but we have done too little to assure that pastors will be qualified educational leaders, particularly in the seminaries.

The basic concepts of religious faith and action are relational. We speak negatively of people who sin, are alienated, lost, or separated. We speak positively of people who are forgiven, reconciled, restored to community with God and other persons, redeemed, saved. We speak affirmatively of those who love, commit themselves, belong, are made whole. God is understood in verbal and relational terms as a process which creates, transforms, and makes new those who are out of line with God's aim. In and through our relationship with God, we become fully human as persons in relationship with other persons. When we think of the church in terms of *koinonia,* as a fellowship of the spirit, we have in mind the quality of life in a relational community in which God is especially but not exclusively active. The local parish seeks to be this kind of community, and we seek God's grace, the free gift of the spirit, as the nucleus of an organically related community.

Such a community is educationally viable, for education by one definition is what happens to a person in community. There is a nurturing process that occurs through what might be called osmosis where the sense of belonging is a powerful influence. The learning is not primarily conscious but is more of an assimilation of ways of doing things, finding richness in rituals and symbols that have meaning for the community. But only as one feels a part of the community are these influences helpful; this kind of nurturing is not a spectator sport.

Key Educational Levels

The community is responsible for the education of its members, whether this be family, church, school, or nation. The sense of belonging, as we have said, is essential, and attempts to incorporate those who are alienated often lead to failures in any level of education. These levels of education might be described as follows:

(1) *Nurture* is the involvement of the pupil in the atmosphere and relations of a community, including knowledge about it as a means toward loyalty to it. Christian nurture is the inclusion of the total person in all the relationships of life from the perspective of participation in the Christian community. This view derives from Horace Bushnell, but is also evident in some theories of socialization. We see it operating most clearly in the family, but it also is evident in various types of team sports, in social groupings and gangs, and in schools and churches. When the nurturing process is positive, the result is an increase of loyalty within the group and to whatever transcends the group and commands the group's loyalty. It also may be negative, driving the individual away from the goals of the group and ultimately from the group itself. The quality of life of the group, including its attractiveness to the individual, is part of the goal of Christian nurture.

(2) Closely related to nurture is the concept of education as *initiation* into value attitudes. This process starts with the assumption that there are worthwhile values and that there are processes by which we can transmit these values in intelligible and yet voluntary ways. R.S. Peters suggests that this can be done as a shared exploration of teacher and pupil, and that over a period of time a contagious enthusiasm for certain values can be caught. This can be combined with a critical analysis, so that the values held by the community may be examined carefully and in many cases revised to suit the current situation. This approach requires

an historical perspective, as one studies the emergence of values in the past, especially those which promise new insights by which to face the future. It also necessitates a view of the moral development of persons from infancy to maturity, and we are helped by the researches of Jean Piaget, Lawrence Kohlberg, Norman J. Bull, and others. Christian educators, however, tend to see morality as closely allied with the religious sentiment, although they may recognize that moral development of a high order is possible without reliance on religious categories.

(3) Another way of looking on education is as *a discipline*. Marc Belth distinguishes between education and schooling and sees education as a discipline which may take place within a school. This is the point at which we interpret education as training in the art of thinking, of dealing with the relations between concepts and actions, of learning to analyze distinctions and to recognize false logical moves, of recognizing that no system of beliefs is beyond questioning. The good educator seeks ways of helping the student to raise questions that the student would not think of asking and then to seek answers. This view of education places an emphasis on data, on powers of observation, on manipulating signs and symbols. But it also builds on the past and stresses memory. There can be no such thing as education in a historical or experiential vacuum. The student then becomes free to make one's own inferences and to test them, returning from the experiment either with verifying evidence or with the need to revise or even discard the inferences. There are no preconceived answers in this kind of education, for its success depends on what the student does with it. No one can do the student's believing for him or her.

(4) In order for education to succeed as nurture, initiation, or a discipline in straight thinking, certain *skills* are required. One aspect of education is *training*. If we are to "equip God's people for work in his service," especially if they are to relate to the educational community, they need orientation training which will help them relate to other people and become sensitive to their needs. When the student and teacher learn to participate in community as those who belong, both teaching and learning can

take place. But some skills are necessary for this kind of relating to be successful, and some of the procedures of socialization are helpful at this point. Included under this view also is procedural training, which involves the acquiring of the skills necessary to use the tools of learning, including the use of memory, for without such skills little learning will take place no matter what opportunities are offered.

(5) There is also education as *insight*. In all processes of growth, there are moments of insight or disclosure when everything is seen in a new perspective. A pattern or paradigm is formed which enables us to realign the data and therefore to understand more clearly what the data mean. In all education, teachers need to work in such a way that new insights may emerge, although they cannot be guaranteed as the result of any method; often such moments of enlightenment occur long after exposure to the classroom situation in which the original stimulus was felt. The use of stories with logically odd twists, or words with logically odd qualifiers, may lead to such disclosures, as is suggested in the writings of Ian T. Ramsey. The insight is often followed by a new or deeper commitment. When this discernment and commitment is centered on the person of Jesus Christ, we have a distinctively Christian educational process.

In all of these distinctions of types of education, it should be noted that they can overlap. Furthermore, the student remains free to respond positively or negatively to the stimulus that is provided; the pupil may be passive and accept what is going on, but similar passivity may indicate a lack of response; there may be unpredictable learnings not part of the teacher's goal; there may be long waits for those moments of discernment that come when the light dawns. The student has to do his or her own learning, but not in a vacuum. There are processes which make learning possible, and unless these processes provide opportunities for student response no learning will take place.

Programming is a way of providing opportunities for learning, and these opportunities must be conceived pluralistically both in terms of the processes and of the students' aptitudes. Although all learning follows certain procedures, no two students learn in the same way or at the same speed. Even the simplest type of training procedures, as for example in an athletic team, must be varied to take account of the aptitudes of the players. Because learning is individualized, the particular goals must take account of the growing edge of each pupil. Education can take place anywhere and through the use of any method, although our theological presuppositions may cause us to emphasize one aspect more than another and in some cases to discard some methods and goals.

What I hope for in the future, therefore, is a religious education program that takes account of the variety in human response, the freedom of the pupil to choose, to grow at his or her own rate, and to respond to those moments of discernment or disclosure that will lead to deeper and fuller commitments. This may come from a continuation of many things we are now doing, if we do them more effectively; but it will also stem from future experiments, some of which are not yet clear or available to us; and also from insights into the findings of theological and educational experimentation.

Theology

For many years I have claimed that theology is a crucial factor in determining the nature of religious education. Which theology one holds determines many of the assumptions, goals, and methods of religious education. What one thinks about God indicates what we can do about education. What one thinks about the nature of the teacher or pupil, or about human nature as such, affects the selection of content, methods, and limits of education. What one thinks about revelation affects the reliance on biblical or church authority, the limitations on freedom to do one's own thinking, and ultimately on the distinction between education, indoctrination, and evangelism. This point is not always clear, and therefore many educational theories have a covert theological position that is evident only after careful analysis. How we answer the question "What does it mean to be human?" involves also what we think about the nature of God and the nature of reality, and education is always concerned with the fulfillment of human potentialities.

In recent years, theological assumptions have surfaced in both Catholic and Protestant resource materials, determining both content and method. Usually this has been accomplished by competent educators who recognize that theology and education are independent disciplines in dialogue with each other, rather than establish either as dominant. Therefore, for example, in the writings of George Albert Coe we find a dialogue between the theology and educational theory of Coe and the philosophy and educational theory of John Dewey, leading to an impressive theory of religious education. But the impact of Barthian theology in the late 1930's and early 1940's led to a dissolution of the prior dialogue, and educational theory was altered.

The problem today is to develop both theology and educational theory to meet the current situation and to anticipate the future. We interpret the world in a new way, against the background of evolution, mathematical physics, the principle of indeterminacy, and an organic overall view of reality. Thus we are separated from the ways of thinking in the fourteenth, sixteenth, and nineteenth centuries, where some church theologies are still located. We are training children and adults to live even beyond the twentieth century into the twenty-first. They need the tools, knowledge, and methods to live meaningfully in a new kind of world that is faced with almost insuperable problems in such areas as ecology, energy, racism, feminism, sexism, overpopulation, and probably mass starvation.

One option is to take seriously process theology as a view of the nature of things that may prove valid in the future. This way of thinking uses as a primary model the human body, which is interrelated and organic, is in its parts constantly becoming and perishing, and yet has a continuing identity until death. The human being is a superior actual entity related to other actual entities in all kinds of ways, from the inorganic to the organic. The human person comes to actuality in relation to other persons, develops genuine freedom for conscious choice and action, is capable of moral responsibility, and understands itself as having worth. There is a *will to belong* which leads to a sense of community, provides consensus on the meaning of life and provides the basis for survival.

Human beings are aware of their surroundings in a variety of ways. They begin by having a strong sense of the whole, a sense which involves deep feelings and sometimes conscious awareness. From the whole they abstract sense data pointing to particulars. They respond by means of the whole body with acts of commitment, with appreciation of value, with the worship of God. There is a grasping of the reality of what is other than the person, as well as an inner grasping of one's own bodily processes. And so they come to know. They have a kind of empathy for others, a feeling of their feelings, a mutual interpenetration. It is a vague affective tone, which Whitehead called a "prehension." We can prehend God, who also prehends us. "You will know that I am in my Father, and you in me, and I in you" (Jn 14:20).

Human beings become aware of God, primarily through solitary experiences which sometimes seem to be mystical and which certainly point to what William James called "a mystical germ." There is a sense of wonder, with a response in terms of duty and reverence and the rightness of things. Whatever is the reality behind such an experience, our beliefs are vindicated by a return to the community which shares such beliefs.

In process theology, the God who is experienced is fitted into a coherent system of thought. God is everlasting as a potential source of values not yet realized; God is immanent as persuasive love prehending all that becomes and perishes, taking it into God's own nature. In this view, God shares our suffering and joys and is altered by them, so that we no longer think of God as incapable of passion or change.

Central to this view is that if God is persuasive love, the element of coercion is reduced to some form of judgment. There is room for our experiences of change, of chance, of the emerging of novelty, of freedom. We become in some real and significant sense co-creators with God of the world we live in, and yet the process is always in danger of sinking into chaos. The presence of chance is essential to the possibility of the emergence of novelty, which is the actualizing of values.

From the religious point of view, this way of looking on God allows for the appearance of evil as something opposed to God. Evil is not good in disguise, suffering is not a force to make people good. Evil is a brute force which causes suffering, and God shares that suffering. There is no pious claim that God causes or permits suffering for our own good. Evil remains evil, suffering remains suffering. God shares in our suffering, as one who understands, just as God shares our joys.

God has a purpose for the universe, and especially for human beings. The purpose of religion is to assist in aligning our aims with those of God. We can discover that it is God's purpose that human beings live together in community, as a body with diverse members. God's aim is in the area of aesthetics, broadly interpreted, for true community means true harmony, and harmony is something to be enjoyed. If we are to "have life abundantly," this points to the richness of experience in the "joy and peace of believing." This is where we find the kingdom of heaven. This view of community becomes the basis for understanding the nature of the church.

A deity so understood is both incarnational and sacramental. If God is in the world and the world in God, there is a principle of immanence that is central. There is an ingression of God into the world processes. As the principle of concretion, God limits the process so that it does not become chaos. As a persuasive force of love, God provides a lure of feeling to draw human beings more fully into God's orbit. We can say in traditional terms that God was incarnate in Jesus as the Logos and remains present with us as Holy Spirit or the presence of God or Christ, and we find God sacramentally through baptism and the Lord's Supper.

Even before we ask about the implications in this theology for worship or education, we need to remind ourselves that such a theology can help us understand some recent developments. If we are concerned with racism, and especially black theology, we are alerted to the fact that a process theology does not depend on religious images derived from Western culture. The idea of a despotic deity derived from Egyptian, Greek, and Roman models is discarded. Religious art that depicts the white male as supreme becomes only a cultural artifact. The theses of black theology about evil, liberation, and freedom are supported. If we are concerned with sexism, we can begin by recognizing that images of God are only analogies from dominant aspects of a male dominated culture, and that female images or nonsexist images are just as valid. By recognizing that when images or analogies or models are taken literally we are guilty of idolatry, we are freed from distortions that deny full humanity and therefore equality to those of other races and sexes. Theology is enabled to deal with the oppressed in any situation and to become true to the insights about the mission to the poor, the lame, the blind, and the oppressed in the gospel record.

Furthermore, process theology comes to terms with ecology. It sees the whole of reality as a single organism, and therefore nature is not something to be exploited. Human beings do not dominate nature, for they are parts of it and have responsibility for it. Such a position differs from the traditional position that human beings are lords of nature and free to use it in any way whatever. This is not a new insight, but it has been latent in Christianity.

Many Christians and Jews have accepted such goals in the areas of racism, sexism, oppression, and ecology, but they have not always had a theological base consistent with their moral insights. The World Council of Churches, in particular, has been sensitive to human needs at these levels, which has placed it under suspicion among churches dominated by white, male, Western members and leaders. Papal encyclicals have expressed concern in these areas also, but again there has not been an official theology consistent with such humane goals. Process theology is now being understood by both Catholics and Protestants as providing a basis for such understanding.

Worship

The first implication for religious education, if we take process theology seriously, is that worship stands at the center of the response to the religious vision. Whitehead has said that "the power of God is the worship he inspires." If we are to become sensitized to the aim of God, of the "commanding vision," we must start with worship. Here is where we find the ground of hope, even in the midst of so much that seems to deny such optimism.

Worship is related to what happens in solitary awareness of deity, for in worship the individual shares with a community in the prehension of God and of God's prehension of the worshiper, and the individual prehends others as they prehend God. The good news is seen as the possession of the community and as universal in its application. Thus one's personal prehension of God is strengthened by one's prehensions of others who are also in the act of worship.

This corporate experience is similar to those at political rallies, except that the primary focus is on God. There are many minor focal points in worship, such as the celebrations of births, confirmations, weddings, and deaths, which bring to light both the sense of togetherness and the vividness of God's presence. There is a sense of the holy in such experience.

In worship, memory and hope belong together. This is particularly true of the sacrament of Holy Communion, in which the memory of the Last Supper is brought to bear on the present and points to the unknown future with hope. We recall the past which has perished but which is prehended everlastingly by God, and in our prehension of God the past becomes alive as the basis for our present. The emergent novelty which came into actuality in the life of Jesus and is everlastingly prehended by God becomes available to us through the sacrament. Thus we see more clearly the suffering and persuasive love of God in our lives.

Worship includes preaching and teaching, for the "commanding vision" needs to be pointed to, and most of us need help in seeing what is required. We have inherited a great tradition, including the records of those who have had the most significant insights and have lived according to them. Worship is the basis for reflection on our visions of what it means to be a great person as well as on the presence of God.

Educationally, worship is related primarily to nurture, although the other aspects of education we have described have their parts. In the future, I hope to see families and persons of all ages sharing in worship that is geared theologically to the flexibility of ritual that process thought requires, pointing to an adventure of the spirit that involves risk rather than safety. Children belong in worship when they feel themselves as persons who share in the community. It is possible to achieve this if we who control the forms and practices of worship are sensitive to children and their presence.

Teaching

Teaching emerges from the community that is held together by worship. This is why I am primarily concerned with the kind of education we have in churches and synagogues, although teaching *about* religion is a responsibility of schools. Education *into* religion is different in purpose, for it is the work of a religious community. I suggest that there is a framework for such teaching, a kind of teaching which should be present as fully as possible in future religious education.

First, those who teach need to realize that a civilization stands or falls on the strength of its religious nucleus. This is a finding of historians such as Toynbee, but Whitehead says it is an "inexorable law" that there must be some transcendent aim or life becomes meaningless for individuals and nations and ultimately for civilizations.

Second, we need to take seriously the phrase in the Lord's Prayer about daily bread. One cannot teaching anything in the area of religion to those who are denied the bodily requirements of food, clothing, and shelter. It is true that Christianity has provided hope for the oppressed throughout the ages, but they need at least a minimum sense of worth even to respond to teaching about God.

Third, there is need for a balance between compulsion and freedom. This is ordinarily a social problem, expressing the contrary needs of order and freedom. Coordination is essential for any degree of social efficiency and therefore for community, but it is the tendency of governing bodies, whether of nations or churches, to go beyond the limits necessary and to usurp power. This same distinction is essential for the welfare of smaller social units such as the family.

Fourth, and most important, is the recognition that the way of persuasion is the basis for all community living and for teaching. In cases of oppression, persecution, or denial of liberty, one learns in order to survive, as a response to coercion and the denial of the sense of worth. When teaching is a positive basis for learning, persuasion is at the center of the process, and freedom of response by those who have a sense of their worth is what makes the difference.

Fifth, behind all four previously-mentioned aspects is the sense of a persuasive and loving God, toward whom one's reverence increases through experiences of worship and reflection on all kinds of experience. One comes to the conclusion that there are processes working for the good of humankind, that there are ways of being transformed, that creative advances into novelty take place within us, and that we have worth in the sight of God.

These five points, we have suggested, provide the presuppositions by which the religion teacher must guide the educational course.

Who, then, should teach? In my view of the future, I would start with the admonition of James: "Let not many of you become teachers, my brethren, for you know that we who teach shall be judged with greater strictness" (Jm. 3:1). I would recruit my teachers carefully, looking first for a contagious enthusiasm that reflects the "commanding vision." I would look for someone who is capable of expressing the persuasive love of God to the pupils, who is flexible and open to the needs and yearnings of the pupils, and who is capable of learning along the lines suggested in this essay. It is obvious that this would require a kind of maturity not found in teenagers or in the dogmatic and fixed personalities of any age. Beyond this, I would look for some expertness in teaching skills based on imagination, but this, I think, can be taught with adequate programs of teacher training.

In this process, I would incorporate parents, especially as we deal with younger children. Programmatically, this would mean that parents must be involved in some aspects of the educational process, especially in the period prior to the child's use of language when parents are the primary educators. In many churches, the enlistment of parents can accompany their request for the baptism of the child. Classes for parents of all ages could be provided in any educational program, along with the opportunity for families to worship together along the lines we have described.

We have already alluded to the problem of the morale and enthusiasm of the community that educates, but we need to underscore the point. One can say that the education a person receives or gains depends on the quality of life of the educating community, but this morale develops over a long period of time and the process cannot be programmed except for minor experiments in group process or certain kinds of pastoral teamwork by the laity. What may be the most important educational move one can make is to insist on the deeper theological meaning of the ministry of the laity. If this insight is evoked in enough members of a congregation, it can lead to a high level of commitment to the lay ministry both within and outside the congregation. Within, it means a high level of cooperation, morale, and enthusiasm, and thus the learners of every age learn that they belong to a dynamic community given to the persuasive love of God and they are ready for commitment to the reality of God and to a way of life deemed consistent with God's aims.

One of the chief actors in such a drama is the pastor, whose role is similar to that of the principal in a school. The pastor cannot establish such a sense of community, but he or she can become the means or the symbol of what such a community can mean. And when morale begins to build, the pastor can be a factor in sustaining it. Negatively, the pastor has the power to destroy whatever educational processes may reflect the quality of life we are discussing, and this happens far too often. So we need a succession of pastors who are not only trained as educators and administrators of educational programs, but who place education high in their lists of priorities. When this happens, what seem to be miracles may occur.

Goals

If we conceive of the locale of religious education as a dynamic, flexible, and forward-looking community of learners and teachers, what kinds of goals do we seek?

Rather than outline specific goals in terms of description, what we need are areas in which generalized goals may be established. If we take a pluralistic and flexible view of the meaning of religious maturity, we cannot expect results in terms of fixed beliefs or codes of behavior. If we take seriously the meaning of human freedom responding to specific and vague stimuli, both human and divine, we may hope to evoke insights but we cannot determine assembly line results. There may be strong influences at work in various kinds of educational systems, and one may be able to tell the difference between graduates of Catholic, Protestant, and Jewish schools. A student who participates in a process governed by the assumptions of fundamentalism and literalism can be distinguished from one who has been influenced by process theology and the freedom of belonging to a community where a value-loaded quality of life is experienced.

The first goal of religious education in the future ought to be in the area of *attitudes*. The concept of "the mind of Christ" is translated in terms of disposition, spirit, or attitude. "Have the same attitude Christ had" provides a model that is free from any claim to specific imitation, yet points to a way of life that may prove attractive to many learners. It is an attitude of concern and respect for others, based upon a commanding vision of what it means to love. If we are persuaded to love God and to love others as ourselves, we are dealing with an attitude toward the whole of life.

Obviously, talking about such ideas may be helpful, but they do not become educationally effective unless there is opportunity to experience what love means. This takes us back to early childhood, where the experience of being loved and of loving is prior to the development of language. What we need are "words to tell our loving" and not words about love. We need educational processes in terms of being initiated into a value-loaded process of living, being introduced to human models of what love means in action, being placed in situations (either actually or imaginatively) where we can experience love and show love. We also need educational processes in terms of the evoking of insight, for there may be moments of disclosure followed by commitment that come from stories or logically odd formations of language that cause the light to dawn. We certainly need educational processes geared to nurture, for the experience of love is found primarily in limited nurturing communities such as family, church, synagogue, and informal groupings.

The enjoyment of beauty is an essential attitude. Religion leads to the promotion of harmony throughout the whole of the universe, and when the individual experiences harmony it leads to happiness or blessedness. The enthusiasm of believers, who are aware that they are filled with God's presence, enables them to be happy even when they lack the world's goods. They enjoy life, are assured that God enjoys their enjoyment, and in turn they enjoy God's enjoyment of themselves. Thus, religion has transcendent importance. Religious education at its best is thoroughly enjoyable.

A systematic development of attitudes would involve us in a taxonomy of learning, in which we could work toward those which extend from that of love to other forms of behavior. This carries us into the area of religious ethics, both personal and social. It is at this point that attitudes express themselves in specific behaviors.

Before we look at the ethical implications, however, there are two other generalized goals at which we must look briefly.

The second goal of religious education, in this view, should be the establishment of *relationships*. At this point we derive help from the writings of Martin Buber and Reuel Howe. The understanding of the "I-thou" relationship is crucial to religious development. It is through relationships that human beings learn not only the meaning of love and respect for persons, but it is also the way in which we understand God at work in our midst. Many concepts are communicated through what has been called the language of relationships, and therefore the control of relationships within educational communities is an essential factor.

Good teaching depends upon the mutual trust between pupil and teacher. Only as the teacher is seen as a person who cares does the student learn to ask, as Buber puts it, and then relationships can be examined and explained. The emphasis is on education as nurture within the community in which the quality of life makes trust possible. But it also takes skill to enter into relationships, and we can assist students to develop skills that lead to socialization. These skills sometimes are simply to help the pupils get along, which is a form of other-directedness or sometimes tradition-directedness, both of which have their dangers; but also these skills may emerge from an inner-directedness or autonomy leading to a kind of maturity that is one of the end results of good religious education.

Out of the development of such attitudes and relationships we may hope that students will reach maturity, "the full measure of development which belongs to the fullness of Christ, instead of remaining immature, blown from our course and swayed by every passing wind of doctrine, by the adroitness of men who are dextrous in devising error; we are to hold by the truth, and by our love grow up wholly unto him" (Eph. 4:13b-15, Moffatt's translation).

The third goal for religious education in the future is in the area of *content*. At this point we move into the use of education as a discipline. The whole tradition of Christian teaching is open to the most careful examination, so that we may determine what and how we believe in terms congenial to today's world. This means that we must reject all inert ideas which are unable to operate effectively in our lives, make use of the skills utilized in the art of critical thinking, and work out our own views with fear and trembling and yet with a confidence in our own worth as free human beings.

My hope is that many will see fit to work out a system of beliefs consonant with empirical and process theology, and that our educational approach might be geared to such a paradigm for the purpose of examining the data. When successful, this approach will lead to moments of insight, the evoking of a disclosure of the whole in the light of the data that can break the old paradigm and lead to the new one.

The problem is to develop beliefs that are consistent with our view of the world as derived from all sources, especially science. We think as secular persons in terms of the work-a-day world, and, although our religious convictions stand against that world in many ways and pronounce judgment upon it, there needs to be a connection between religious thinking and the secular world or religion will become irrelevant. We need to develop beliefs by which we can evaluate our personal and social behaviors, account for the religious feelings we have, and explain the transformations in human beings that occur due to the reality of deity for which the word God stands. We need to make distinctions in the categories of language we use, so that our communication will be received, for when we mix illegimately the literal and the nonliteral linguistic forms we get nothing but confusion.

The problem with content in any philosophical or theological system is twofold. Educationally, we are tempted to work for premature conclusions among younger pupils, and thus there is fixation long before mature concepts are possible. This is closer to indoctrination than to education, and the teacher or pastor becomes a source of answers rather than one who equips pupils to think things through. But both of these dangers, premature conclusions and indoctrination, lead to assumptions of exactness, and any claim of exactness in theology is a fake. We may be sure that we are in some kind of relation with a reality we call God, but this does not entail certainty of belief. The whole point of theological exploration is that it is open-ended, that there are new ways of arranging the data of religion so that our overall view is under constant revision. Education is always a reexamination of the evidence in the light of new ways of looking on the world, and remains an exciting and unique experience for us all.

The fourth goal for religious education in the future is in the area of *personal morality*. The earliest Christians were known as followers of the way. They were not distinguished from others by language, clothing, or manners, but by their working to hold the world together. They not only loved each other, but they loved those outside the fold, although this led to opposition from the government and from other religious groups. The level of personal morality and of noncooperation with the government was such that they could be distinguished and therefore persecuted. There were some groups of Christians who felt so free from the law that they became or remained corrupt, but the overall impression we get is a somewhat idealized picture of moral individuals in a closely knit community.

Today, in the light of research into moral development, the conclusion is that moral education can operate effectively outside the domain of religious membership or belief, but this has always been recognized and should not disturb us. Our problem is with the development of moral behavior within the Christian community, in which beliefs about the nature of God and of human beings issue in moral behavior. Religion is significant not because of its moral claims so much as because of its supreme importance for the meaning of living, and when a child goes to Sunday school in order to learn how to be good, we have a distortion of Christian teaching.

Augustine said that we should love God and do as we please. This sounds like dangerous license from a secular viewpoint, but it points to the freedom that we have under God. It assumes that if we love God we will love our neighbor. Love is understood as a commitment or responsibility that provides only general directives and not specific ones. The same is true of other general values, such as beauty, justice, goodness, and temperance. The ethical problem is to relate general directives to specific situations.

We can be helped in our understanding of a religiously based moral education by the realization that a moral imperative requires a total response, not just will or emotion or intellect but a combination that is total. The primary attitude is respect and concern for persons, but we must also be aware of the emotions on all sides, the knowledge of the possible consequences, the capacity to bring about some practical end, the ability to make a decision, and the act itself. (See John Wilson et al, *Introduction to Moral Education,* Penguin, 1967, pp. 190–195). Jean Piaget and Lawrence Kohlberg have shown how persons move through various stages of moral judgment. Our task is to use this knowledge within the framework of membership in the religious community.

We would hope for a religiously based moral education that is not restricted to concepts of law and order, or even to the Ten Commandments, but which operates in general terms of love, justice, and truth. In the process of moral growth, we would expect to use moral rules and apply various forms of law and discipline, but we would move forward rapidly to the use of freedom and responsibility within the framework of more generalized principles, arriving at the end at an autonomy of moral judgment which is a genuine exercise of freedom.

A fifth area in which goals of a future religious education must be defined is *social ethics*. This is a false distinction, for any responsibility for personal behavior involves social imperatives as well, but traditional Christianity has often made the distinction. Two passages serve to underscore the social implications of the teachings of the gospel. One is the excerpt from the Magnificat:

> He has put down the mighty from their thrones,
> and exalted those of low degree;

> he has filled the hungry with good things,
>> and the rich he has sent empty away.
>
> (Lk. 1: 52–53)

The other is Jesus' quotation from Isaiah in the synagogue at Nazareth:

> The Spirit of the Lord is upon me,
>> because he has anointed me to preach the good news
>> to the poor.
> He has sent me to proclaim release to the captives
>> and recovering of sight to the blind,
> to set at liberty those who are oppressed,
>> to proclaim the acceptable year of the Lord.
>
> (Lk. 4: 18–19)

We find in these words a radical view of social justice which threatens all privilege and identifies the aim of God with the concerns of the outcast, oppressed, hungry, and poor. It is a poignant message that is likely to be rejected by those in the churches, and to be resented when inserted into a program of religious education. The distinction between righteousness and unrighteousness is seen at the political, economic, and social level. Thus, God's subjective aim is understood in terms of the achievement of community on a global scale, and the Christian is asked to align his or her aims with this general aim of God. The potential for social justice lies in those eternal forms by which God is guided, and the persuasive love of God seeks to move us in this direction. Only then may we speak meaningfully of the kingdom of God.

Educationally, we run into a stalemate at this point. Grass-root churches which are happy to portray personal morality as a requirement, although often at the level of moralism or "being good," are incapable of rising above the assumptions and ethical insights of the society in which they operate. Church members are not likely to be in the advance guard of those working for civil rights, racial harmony, open housing, or the liberation of oppressed groups, although they will respond with sympathy to crises of hunger and suffering in specific cases. But the church is more than a local congregation. It expresses its nature also in ecumenical gatherings, and this is where the prophetic tradition of the Jewish and Christian scriptures have remained alive and relevant. Our religious education programs need to widen their scopes to include what is coming from the World Council of Churches and the National Council of Churches, as well as from ecumenical Catholic documents on social justice.

We have said that process theology includes in its scope our concerns about nature, ecology, racism, sexism, and other current issues. Thus, there can be a reformation in theology that provides a basis for social ethics. If all living things are interrelated in a dynamic and evolutionary process, our responsibility as human beings is to the earth as we have inherited it and to the welfare of all actual entities. If God is both the potential for future values and the loving presence that encourages us to make those values actual, we can hope that human aims may be aligned with God's overall aim for humanity. An education grounded in worship and seeking the goals we have briefly mentioned may move in the direction of the kingdom of heaven on earth.

CONCLUSION

My view of the future provides no blueprint, no significant program, no advance into new methods. I have been thinking primarily of religious education in church and family. The possibilities of method, locale, and content have been on the whole been left open, because flexibility is the key to my hope for the future, which I see as open-ended. If all life is becoming and perishing, and each becoming builds on what has perished, we need to take advantage of emerging novelty as it becomes actual. The creative influence of God remains everlastingly at work, but even God may be surprised—for good or ill. And so may you and I.

CHAPTER III

Restoring the Whole Word for the Whole Community

Carl F. H. Henry

The Present from Which the Future Flows

When Jesus who said, "I am the way, the truth and the life; no man cometh unto the Father but by me," defined the first and greatest commandment as "Thou shalt love the Lord thy God with all thy heart, and with all thy soul, and with all thy mind," and added the second, "Thou shalt love thy neighbour as thyself," he gave us the ground, motivation, and objective not only of Christian education, but of life itself, namely, divine authority, the commandment of love, and personal and social worth through spiritual renewal.

Today's existential concerns relate specifically to these matters of authority, motivation, and purpose: Who am I? Why am I here? Am I responsible to anyone? Am I responsible for anything? What is the good life? How can I obtain it? Is this life all there is? Some forty years ago the assigned topic for my first college English theme was "Why I Am Here"; in that day those words assumed not unresolved questions but rather resolved declarations about spiritual realities and human purpose. In the present quarrel with life those exclamations have skewed into question marks.

The Washington Post in the mid-1970's profiled some young people who had left the "provinces" to "find themselves." One of those whose life now revolves around a $13,000 government job, parties with "name" people, a morally experimental existence inside and outside her $300 apartment, and a lover from New York

15 years her senior and married, had this to say: "I think the trouble with my generation is that with all the freedom, the lack of guilt, we don't have any ground rules, nothing to fall back on in the middle of the revolution. I guess we're having to make our own rules as we go along." Apparently those self-made rules provide neither satisfying experiences, nor the ability to cope with life in general. Speaking more symbolically than she knew of many lonely, unsuccessful associates, this runaway from a church and family-oriented home added: "There seemed to be a farewell party every day."

What has surfaced so boldly in recent years is not anything particularly new, of course. Ever since Adam, man has tried to come to grips with himself, with his environment, his world, his destiny. Nor have man's varied efforts to answer his questions differed substantially from age to age and generation to generation. To matter numerically in a world of four billion souls— perhaps eight billion by the year 2000—is a concern, but not the first of man's concerns. Of greater concern are the intensity and omnipresence of threats to personal worth in a gargantuanly chaotic world. How is one to pick the sure, let alone the right path through or from this spinning vortex of commingled justice and injustice, truth and falsehood, purity and impurity, honesty and dishonesty, peace and war, freedom and license, ambition and greed, respect and abuse—the list grows daily in one's exposure to man's attacks upon himself in grubbing for survival and power. There is no stopping the ears to epithets of frustration; there is no closing the eyes to the scarred nudity of our times. Perhaps unwillingly but nonetheless surely, man is learning that he has never been nor can he be an island; he is newly being forced to accept if not to learn that there are indeed no islands whatever to be had, personal or otherwise, in which to indulge either his perverseness or, for that matter, his saintliness. Man needs to count to himself, that least common denominator of existence from which, through which and to which his life ebbs and flows from birth to death. However long or short, that interval unremittingly challenges his self-orientation until at some point he either acknowledges the fact of *imago dei* and its implications, or continues life-long to deny it and to fight against its pricks.

The Basic Task of Christian Education

Christian education properly conceived and implemented will, in the future, speak increasingly more pointedly to this harassment of the *imago dei,* and to be heard and heeded in a science-, sex-, and security-oriented world is its staggering responsibility. Obviously these three fascinations are not to be repudiated nor condemned per se, but to allow millennial expectations for them is quite another matter. Christianity has never truly been antiscience, antisex nor antisecurity; what it has been and continues to be is pro-the Christ, incarnate God, Savior Lord, Coming Judge and King of kings who said, "I am come that they might have life, and . . . have it more abundantly." Convinced that only the God-related, reborn person understands what life—abundant life—is, Christian education dedicates itself to fashioning that new person in Jesus Christ. Its content, methodology, environment, scope, and overall procedure will revolve around that objective.

But just who is this new person in Jesus Christ? Evangelical Christianity future no less than present and past answers this question according to biblical formulations. I remember still that when I was a young editor on Long Island an elderly widow, a proof reader, one day politely removed her glasses, looked intently at me and said, "Carl, you must be born again. Jesus said that, you know, and He knew more about spiritual things than anyone else." The new person in Jesus Christ is "dead unto self, alive unto God"—he is "born again," words that Jesus addressed to even Nicodemus, a rabbi and theologian. Confession of and repentance for sin and identification with Christ in His death and resurrection usher whosoever wills to believe into reconciliation and peace with God, membership in the Church, Christ's Body through whom He functions, and empowerment by the imparted and indwelling Holy Spirit to know and do God's will for His glory and honor. Call it what you will—being born again, becoming a child of God, becoming a new creation in Christ—all, not incidentally, biblical descriptions—this transaction by grace through faith is a part of God's redemptive plan for man and the universe.

This consciously willed commitment is but the first but essential step in a lifetime of growth into conformity to Jesus Christ and into wholeness of love toward God and neighbor. Learning to love God with one's whole being—or more explicitly, allowing "Christ in us, the hope of glory" to work Himself out in and through us becomes the hallmark of the maturing Christian who properly understands what self-realization is in his own experience and in society. Stuntedness, unfortunately, characterizes much of so-called Christianity, so that the Christian faith is bypassed or canceled out as a live option for meeting personal and social dilemmas.

The Church is often charged with apathy and loss of caring, and additionally, with lack of discipline. Does the latter perhaps explain the former? After all, the new person in Jesus Christ, if functioning fully under divine authority according to God's commandment of love will not only fulfill himself but will also bless the world around him and by so doing will convincingly attract others into the Way that provides satisfying answers to life's problems. Malcolm Muggeridge once wrote in the *Christian Inquirer,* ". . . unless men have a sense of moral order within themselves and in their universe, they will not be able to build any other kind of order, economic, political, or social."

Ever increasing secularization and ever increasing religious pluralism will make the future task of the Church and of Christian education within it staggeringly complex, and certainly difficult. Be that as it may, a Christianity that attracts the searching, often cynical but honest secularist, agnostic, or even atheist is one that usually convinces first of all not by argument or program but by lifestyle. Of the early Christians it was said, "See, how they love one another." In other words, the relevant practice of biblical truths and concepts in family, community, industry, business, and government as well as in church life lifts Christian identification from the low status of something "inherited" and socially, even economically and politically desirable—that is to say, an item in one's vita—to its proper category of a live, functioning personal relationship to God. When the implications of this new life in Christ are thoroughgoingly and winsomely lived out in all areas of human conduct, public and private, then we have the biggest and best program of Christian education available. In other words, every person identified with the Christian cause or who attaches to himself the name of Christian "sells" Christ and the biblical message as either necessary and desirable or as dispensable and irrelevant. Unless Jesus Christ and His Good News become the nuts and bolts and glue of daily living, modern pragmatic man will simply hang on to other alternatives however unsatisfying, mercurial, even devastating they may be. It is the wedding of Jesus Christ with every aspect of daily living that must be the hallmark of any Christian education of the future which merits the term "Christian."

As I see it, the worst by-product of modern technology is the secular-city mentality that debunks the supernatural, projects an earthly utopia where Jesus Christ is an irrelevance, and promotes social revolution to achieve it. The early Christians identified the destiny of life in supernatural dimensions. Created for a destiny in eternity, man needs the mediatorial work of Jesus Christ to join the fellowship of the regenerate and to lend durable meaning and worth to the social order. Only the new birth and new life in Christ can restore life to what God intends. Human existence rests not simply upon the past and present, but upon God's purpose in the future as well. Evangelical Christianity needs to identify for the modern world the criteria by which God wants men and nations to live, and for whose transgression they will be judged. The first disciples witnessed justification and justice to their world not simply in obedience to Jesus, but also because the fact and significance of the eternal world were compellingly real to them. They knew Jesus who lived a perfect life among them, who died a sacrificial death among them, who appeared in resurrection triumph among them, and who ascended from their midst with the promise of return. His resurrection disclosed the direction of human history, for He was the firstfruits of a universal resurrection of the dead—each in his own order. The risen Lord was the source and power of their new life, the ground of their hope for the coming King before whom every knee must bow. This conviction constrained and impelled them to witness concerning the Risen One who vanquished the terror of physical and spiritual death, and who gives assurance not only of a final future day of judgment at His throne, but also of power to confront the daily issues of present existence. This is no time to isolate ourselves behind the sandbags of faith while waiting for the world to collapse. Faith must march forward and ransom the future of the world.

The Bible and Christian Education

Jesus brought new clarity and solemnity to the concept of life hereafter, but also of life here and now. The Bible is no mere fair-weather and fair-havens Book; it is a Book for all seasons in a many-seasoned world. Its message is not something finite men have cleverly devised; it is something which the infinite, holy but loving God has been gracious enough to share. It teaches that the most desolating calamities are not physical and external but spiritual and internal. It exposes man's refusal to face priorities. By raising problems, very urgent indeed, of social injustice, communism, scientism, pollution, and so on, the man in flight from God camouflages his primary need, that of soul-surgery. Man's problem is not that he lacks any insight concerning right and wrong but that he lacks the heart or refuses to do even what he does know to be right. He transgresses against God and knows it. How can I do, and be, what I ought? Oh, wretched man that I am, who shall deliver me? is the anguished cry of an honest man. Far too many persons identify God with deliverance, not from personal sin and evil but simply from evil circumstances. Their pleas are for safety but not for the Savior, a cry that denies personal guilt and responsibility. Beyond seeing man suffering through the sins of men, they must come to see God suffering through men's sins, including their own, and Christ bearing them in atoning love on the cross. Christian education of the future must help men experience suffering in a positive, Christian manner.

A Vision for Christian Education

Society disbars lawyers, revokes doctors' licenses, even impeaches presidents whose public or private practice do violence to the respected and expected code of their calling and profession. May it not be that as never before our church constituencies must be held personally responsible for practicing round the clock and seven days a week what they profess on Sunday? As we have said, the biggest and most influential arena for implementing Christian education is found outside of the structural boundaries and formal program of the Church. Church leaders and staff know this. But unless they deliberately and consistently stress and expect the entire Christian fellowship wherever it functions to be the visual embodiment of the Church's technical program of Christian education, charges of outmodedness and irrelevance will continue to blight the Church's efforts. Every committed believer is every day and in every way a participant in either upgrading or debasing the formal program of education and, more than that, the functioning of the living Body of the Lord Christ. This overarching concept of Christian education is no fatuous theory. Far from it. Just as we are called upon to be conformed to the image of Jesus Christ and then proceed by the Spirit to particularize steps of growth toward that conformity, so conscious awareness of one's expected 100% role in Christian-Education-in-Life motivates learning and training toward that end. Before the builder there must be a plan, but before the plan there must be the vision. It is vision which, in the final analysis, will make or break the Christian education of the future.

The determinative vision of Christian education equipping the whole man for all stages and ages of life must incorporate specific content within a specific context. What is to be communicated, by whom, and how, and where? Proclamation by life does not just happen; it is largely the fruit of proclamation of the Word. According to a 1971 Gallup query, "Americans are deeply disturbed about the declining role of religion." Moreover, in Ben Wattenberg's words, "it diminished at just about the time when the 'new' culture dawned, an aggressively anti-traditional culture, an anti-square culture that even seemed to have a branch office in organized religion itself where clergymen preached on Vietnam and racism, burned draft records, and asked, 'Is God dead' all to the beat of Jesus Christ Superstar.'' The Jesus People, an amalgam of great diversity, did much to surface a growing dissatisfaction with this approach, and an undeniable hunger for honest answers and valid guidelines as found in the Bible. (A product of these years, a converted atheist, published a book in France, *La Cadavre de Dieu bonge,* "God's corpse is moving".) They contributed to the explosion of lay-oriented Bible study groups that reverberated across the United States (and many parts of the world) and that said, in part: "The institutional church puts us off. Let's study among ourselves where we are, just the way we are. Let's learn how to pray and to help one another." Today the Bible no longer waits patiently for discovery in religious book stores; it's a well-displayed, hot item in supermarkets and drugstores. Many of the Jesus People are now absorbed into established churches where their present and future contribution (and the church's contribution to them) is constructive. Many have enrolled in Bible colleges and seminaries, not necessarily to train for the technical ministries, but to solidify and deepen their biblical pursuit. Others are seen and heard in social, government, educational, journalistic, musical, athletic, and other circles—unashamed to speak a good word for Jesus Christ and the Bible as authoritative. Meantime the Bible study groups continue and no doubt will, seen not as threats to the institutional church, but as welcome catalysts and reinforcement to the primary business of proclaiming God's Word. Many churches, in fact, see these groups as helpful ways to spread and draw the net of evangelization and nurture in more localities among more people, and are helping to foster and sometimes lead these groups within and outside the church. The lay principle is very important in making the Bible what it is intended to be, a book for everyone's personal perusal and appropriation and not for the ministerium only. It is no longer inconceivable for a layman to chide his pastor for a meager message or to confront him with a "Thus saith the Lord!"

To the question, "Where will the Bible be in the year 2000?" a professor in a marginally related denominational school replied: "Five years ago (1970) when we took a class of freshmen to talk to them about the Bible . . . the first task of the professor was to convince the kids that this is important. It's not true of our undergrads today. It's just the opposite. Five years ago you had to argue with a kid that this is relevant, that he ought to be studying the Bible. Today you've got to argue with him against some form of Bibliolatry. . . . These are the kids who are going to be sitting where you're sitting in ten years. . . . What I see in the current generation of college students is a great deal more conservatism than I knew five years ago . . . they're products of the conservatism that has swept the country. . . ." This observation elicited remembrance of the roadsign: "Utopia Baptist Church, Two Miles on the Right." Many leaders agree that the cleavage between so-called fundamentalist and broader groups will be increasingly apparent 25 years from now. In the midst of growing pluralism there will be a clearer focus on the particularity of the Gospel: that God in Jesus Christ has done not only some new thing but also some once-and-for-all thing in reconciling the world unto Himself.

To meet this growing interest in the Bible—or to capitalize on it—a vast array of study materials is available for all age groups to be used in weekday as well as Sunday gatherings. And to further supplement the earnest student's quest there are even Greek classes for laymen, and theological extension courses. This trend of serious in-depth Bible is growing especially among college-age young people who most keenly face the crunch of antisupernaturalism and dialectical materialism on their campuses. The urgent need in the future is to more and more systematically equip high school and even younger students with convincing supports for their Evangelical faith, and to do so before, not after they encounter devastating pressures. What's more, these young people want not only to stand and withstand in the "evil day," but also to witness effectively to their friends and teachers. As never before the church school and other phases of Christian education must be—and can be, because the interest is there—bona fide situations of purposeful study and learning. It may be, in fact, that in the aftermath of much internalizing of Scripture truth in many of the informal study groups (and exposure to a plethora of Bible translations, versions and paraphrases) that an acute need arises for structured, biblical theology that surmounts the dangers of subjectivism by propounding objective propositional truth. We need once again to lay out the evidences necessary for defending the reliability and the truthfulness, not simply the existential value, of Scripture and Jesus' claims. Students need help in probing the antisupernatural presuppositions that characterize the educational scene and that reject biblical faith. Perhaps as never before "I believe" needs the essential apologetic corollary of "Why I believe." Someone has said, "To have no faith is callousness; to have undiscerning faith is superstitution."

Foundational to any apologetic statement is one's view of Scripture. Evangelical Christianity holds it to be authoritative because divinely inspired; it is therefore truthful and trustworthy. Because Scripture is God's truth it has authority over men as the infallible rule for faith and practice. While God's Word is changeless for all men in all times and places it is not therefore "wooden," however. The same Holy Spirit Who moved and superintended the different writers of the original manuscripts, breathes His comprehension of those writings into the divergent personalities of those who receive God's revelation for what it is. This ever-living, ever-relevant, ever-contemporary significance of Scripture for all time and creation bespeaks its source in the Creator God, and helps to underscore its transracial, transcultural, transnational pertinence.

Because of its foundation in the unique revelation of God, Christianity expounds what it believes to be the only valid world-life view that answers man's questions concerning himself, the world, nature, and history. Christian education therefore involves communicating and articulating as well as demonstrating that world-life view as set forth in Scripture, epitomized supremely in Jesus Christ, Savior and Lord, Coming Ruler and Judge, and proclaimed by His Body, the universal Church. That message is perennially revolutionizing, proffering satisfaction for the runaway heart, home for the drifting spirit, meaning for the jaded intellect, and direction for society as a whole. Christian education functions with the objective that men will not only "entertain" ideas, but will truly "embrace" them. As Gary Hardaway, a juvenile probation officer wrote in *Christianity Today:* "If today I am not increasing in wisdom, spiritual understanding and knowledge of God, I may well be shell-shocked by the explosions of tomorrow. This means I should master the eternal facts and precepts of my faith right now. It means disentangling myself from temporary goals. It means grappling with the spiritual errors of today, diagnosing their ungodly heredity, forseeing their disastrous consequences." Mental inertia in the church, keeping people "babes in understanding" by a perpetual diet of well-diluted milk will provide little spiritual and moral muscle for the days ahead. "God has apprenticed our sons and daughters to us for a few years," Hardaway continues, "not only to learn the skills of discipleship. Our job is to show them how to become journeyman saints, skilled spiritual craftsmen."

The Church becomes spiritually delinquent and doctrinally confused when deprived of Scripture-oriented teaching and preaching. Take the Bible away and you soon take away worship of the living God who reveals Himself, who introduces Himself by name, who speaks His own thoughts and words. Without the Bible the great heritage of faith soon yields to counterfeit religions powerless to define and implement love and law. Collapse of civil society then becomes inevitable, and life loses its meaning. Proclaiming the moral laws by which God rules His created universe, the Bible declares those standards to which men and society must conform if civilization is to endure. To lose the Bible is to lose everything. Man's ultimate choice is to be possessed either by this Book with its driving dedication to the holy will of God, or by the carnal spirit of mammon with its engulfing fires of violence and despair. While the Bible is ot a textbook on science or economics or politics or history, its principles are nonetheless relevant for properly handling these realms in a God-oriented, responsible way. Only an unfractured, unbroken Bible suffices for building and maintaining a viable, permanent faith.

A major task in a viable Christian education of the future is to expose, by biblically based and philosophically valid teaching, the rationalistic prejudices of our times. Being able to give a reason for one's faith and concerning one's faith is indispensable, both to manifest the futility and irrationality of unbelief and to lay bare the coherency of biblical truth. The thesis of intellectual life today, by and large, is that there is no God. To have lost this framework of conviction in our Western society, the controlling idea of a supernatural God, has cast us adrift in all areas of life. Alert to this devastating trend, then president of Harvard Nathan Pusey said to his departing seniors in 1959, "It would seem to me that the finest fruit of serious learning should be the ability to speak the word God without reserve or embarrassment, certainly without adolescent resentment; rather, with some sense of communion, with reverence and joy."

Communion, reverence and joy grow not simply from reading the Bible as good literature, which it assuredly is, or from reading millions of words about the Bible, helpful as this may be. They stem, rather, from personally investigating the Bible as God's holy, infallible, authoritative revelation. Rewarded with newness of life and insight by the Spirit, even the humblest of such investigators outstrips in essential wisdom those who however philosophically and speculatively adept, remain willfully unbelieving of the grace of God and its blessings. Today's most devastating poverty is not lack of material things—it is lack of a working knowledge of God's Word for the whole man. Many of the intellectual giants who are at home in outer space are strangers to the God of creation and the God of redemption and are unable to cope with personal conflict and depravity. Our technological progress has been remarkable, but we have, at the same time, the tools of self-destruction within our unregenerate grasp and manipulation. The Christian believes that the will of God and the prayers of His people can influence the direction of society. The secular historian, on the other hand, limits all explanations of events to this world as we know and fashion it. Will Durant put it this way: "I am descendant of a monkey . . . and so I understand the instincts we suffer from—violent pugnacity, limitless acquisition, indomitable sexual desire" and adds—with tongue in cheek?— that he has lost his faith in "the wickedness of mankind." This sort of evolutionary orientation in the classroom, coupled with indifference to fixed authority and norms of behavior and often outright rejection of biblical faith and the supernatural, leaves thousands of young people in limbo academically and morally. "We . . . were so sure that at long last a generation had arisen, keen and eager," said Walter Lippmann, "to put this disorderly earth to right. . . . We meant so well, we tried so hard, and look what we have made of it. . . . What is required is a new kind of man."

Toward a Refashioning of Objectives

That new kind of man is the new person in Jesus Christ; this must be the primary objective of Christian education in the future, as it should be of Christian education today. What biblical truths can help fashion such a person to stand tall in his generation? An understanding of man's divine origin. The fact of man's willful rebellion against God, consequent sinful nature, and separation from God. God's provision of His only Son—crucified, risen, and ascended—as Savior and Lord, Reconciler, returning Judge and King; The Person of the Holy Spirit indwelling and empowering believers to conform to the image of Jesus Christ. The formation, constituency, and function of the Church. The mandate of the Great Commission to every believer. These basics embodying creation, redemption, the mission of the Church, and eschatology, and their personal and social implications can be taught, ideally should be taught, in sequential stages related to chronological and spiritual maturity for their best cumulative impact.

In our transient, mobile society, few persons, especially in the crucial younger years, have a prolonged continuing exposure to such a program of systematic biblical instruction, unless they are fortunate enough to move where a similar viewpoint and program of Christian education obtains. While the Sunday church school by its very nature probably stays closer to explicit Bible teaching, it is nonetheless vulnerable to materials often furnished by boards or publishing houses and required by denominational spokesmen that minimize the supernatural, emphasize an evolutionary approach to life, and downplay being "born again" as the irreducible point of beginning toward new personhood. It seems to me that the whole area of curriculum needs investigation—for solidity and progression of Scripture content, for respectable confrontation with the speculative tenets of the times, for helps in meeting the challenges to a reasoned faith in daily experience, for principles in formulating practical guidelines in moral and social and interpersonal situations. Curriculum improvement and refining is one of the most important tasks confronting Christian education in the future.

Obviously such specialized curriculum materials require specially equipped writers. We have them, and will continue to have them in the future *if* they see the vision—college, university, and seminary graduates with genuine commitment to Jesus Christ—young people who have personally won their faith through interaction with the thought systems of secular education, who recognize the imperative of discipling and indoctrinating, if you will, prophets for God among what may be the last few generations before Armageddon. The sense of Christian vocation that washes dishes and scrubs floors to the glory of God, that assembles Hondas, feeds computers, plants wheat, collects garbage, votes legislation, anchors TV, strums guitars to the glory of God and the blessing of mankind doesn't emerge overnight. The challenge of such vocational perspective and involvement must be a conscious, continuing concern of the churches and their families. Vocational training begins in the heart and mind and soul loving God; this conviction must be communicated by the Church through its concept of work and Christian calling. As never before the future needs young people especially to penetrate teaching, science, government, the media—all sectors of life—with such professional expertise that their spiritual witness will be readily received. Loving God with one's whole being and one's neighbor as oneself involves dedicating vocational and professional decisions according to the will of God. In this end time curriculum writing for Christ and His cause is a unique opportunity for qualified persons who wish to educate future generations in a truly Christian way.

Such a curriculum, moreover, should be geared and available not only to one phase of the Christian education program like the Sunday School, for example, but should be adaptable also to additional weekday youth and adult activities. Purposeful, cohesive programming around the permeating objective of the new person in Jesus Christ must be more than a whimsical ideal; it is an imperative for future days. If the concept of transdenominational, transcultural, transracial and transnational impact of the Gospel is to function, then the use of comprehensively acceptable helps should be encouraged without fear that denominational, even doctrinal peculiarities will be forfeited—these, if honestly appraised, are, after all, of secondary importance to the distinctives of Evangelical Christianity. Under God Evangelical Christianity in the next years can prove this point with winsome vengeance, if it so wills—and so it must will—lest the world bleed to death even faster from its self-inflicted wounds. There is healing in the Good News if it is articulated intelligently and consistently, and fructified by the Holy Spirit to repentance, regeneration, and renewal.

I have already intimated that Christian education involves far more than the Sunday School, crucial as that is. Compare the overall Church program, if you will, to a wheel. At its center is the hub, that unique purpose for which the organism exists, namely, evangelism and nurture (in their fullest import). The hub also represents those persons identified affirmatively with the Church and its purpose. Beyond the hub is the rim of the wheel symbolizing those outside the Church to be reached. Something, obviously, must join hub to rim and rim to hub. Simply stated, this something is the spokes, the ways of channeling the Church to the unchurched, ways of touching peoples' lives where they are—their needs and interests—because of love for God and love for man, to draw them into newness and reorientation of life through salvation in Christ and His Lordship. The ministries of preaching, teaching, music, worship, fellowship, prayer, recreation, social service, community involvement—the spokes vary in number and diversity—all extend a hand to bridge the gap, sometimes an abyss, that divides the churched from the unchurched. Certain spokes may be added, others removed as needs and situations change. But always each outreach must honestly communicate in its handclasp the identity and identifiability of the hub, lest dilution of the Church's proclaimed and demonstrated message invite collapse of the entire structure. Love outstretched, even God's love, has its requisites for appropriation, and in turn, for reciprocation.

The movement within this functioning wheel is two-directional. Under the leadership and example of pastor and staff, the Church family will exercise its stewardship of time, talents, and resources, human and material, inside the fellowship and outward from the hub toward the larger society. As persons are drawn into the Church program through one or several spokes of appeal or interest (seldom, if ever, through all), they will bring with them into the hub abilities to be captured, sanctified, and incorporated into the existing and ever self-expending organism. This mutual sharing, interdependence, and reinforcement of the members of the Church of which the risen Christ is Head will integrate each person's uniqueness into the Body to the glory of God and the blessing of mankind.

In the future, the working week will be reduced, leisure time will be extended, four-day holidays will be legalized, and Sunday will more and more become a sports and fun day for many persons; therefore the Church will need to adjust its traditional way of thinking. Using all the church facilities during all the week for all kinds of ministry to all age groups representing a vast variety of concerns and burdens as well as interests and hopes, the total program of the Church—it is almost impossible to speak narrowly any more about the educational program as such—can become an important and respected force in the life of any community. So long as its business for King Jesus is not merely humanitarian busyness the Church of the future will prosper in spiritual vigor and clout. The possibilities for welcomed ministries are almost limitless—cradle-roll enrollment of babies, together with mothers' and fathers' classes; child care and studies in Christian family life; weekday nursery school; Christian day school; children's weekly activity clubs (Scouts, Bluebirds, denominational and nondenominational groups); support to ministries like Young Life, Youth for Christ, Child Evangelism, InterVarsity, International Students, Campus Crusade for Christ, the Navigators, Christian Women's Club and others; Church and home gatherings for college, university, and business persons for spiritual encouragement, vocational assistance, social opportunities, community involvement; helps to young married and young parents—winning them back to the Church after an absence, sometimes, since high school days; assisting the middle-aged through the "empty nest" and "idle hands" period; maintaining for the aged a sense of worth despite onslaughts of illness, senility, melancholia, financial problems, isolation, empty days and long nights. Added to these usual and "normal" concerns are opportunities to work with the hospitalized, veterans, prisoners, illiterates, refugees, immigrants, exceptional persons (blind, deaf, retarded, etc.), widows and widowers, the divorced—even a quick overview of a community reveals many different neighbors and their needs. How many and varied are the spokes by which to reach them with neighbor love because of God's love!

Introducing people to the love that passes all understanding, that of Jesus who alone can heal the sin-weary soul, illumine the mind, give courage and hope and His presence on the lonesome road is the greatest privilege, biggest job, and greatest joy there is. Sunday services, weekday prayer meetings and study groups in and outside the Church, visitation, musical groups, missionary meetings, individual and group counseling sessions, day camps and centers, retreats, summer vacation Bible schools, Golden Age clubs, home nursing and meals-on-wheels assistance, telephone hospitality, audio-visual services to shut-ins as well as in regular teaching, library work, sponsored half-way houses, shopping center outreach, literacy work, home tutoring, crafts and rehabilitation activities, physical fitness—no one who loves God with his whole being need be idle, nor in fact can or is likely to be with such a whitened harvest of opportunities at the Jerusalem doorstep. None of us can minister to all the problems of all the world, but each of us has at least one candle to shine for Jesus right where we are. That is integral to Christian education. All aspects of the Church, some more than others, but all nonetheless, must make plain and visible the purpose of all this expended time and energy and substance, that is, the indispensability of Jesus Christ as Savior and Lord for a life that is truly life.

Putting the Vision into Action

How shall such a vast program of the future be administered? That depends, in part, on how much of the total venture a particular church will choose to sponsor. It is quickly obvious but it ought to be much more so, that churches need each other to supplement and complement one another's reach and outreach. The time is long past when each one tries to do everything; no one has all the necessary manpower, money and equipment to carry out successfully so large a schedule of work. By joining forces and making qualified leadership available to a number of congregations and by mutually agreeing on governing principles and practices, the overall impact of ministry will be far more efficient and effective. Just as important, the various church bodies will experience the special joy of cooperating in service not to a specific label but to Christ the Head of the Church universal. Moreover, the eavesdropping, peeking community will see how believers do, indeed, love one another, and how they as a body manifest concern and compassion toward those around them. It could well be that the stated directors of religious education in the separate churches could pool their special strengths, rally the assistance of several supporting leaders in their congregations, and together formulate an area-wide dovetailed program, the whole of which is far stronger than its individual parts. Voluntary, lay co-workers are a special strength in the life of any church. Willingness to serve is not sufficient qualification, however. Personal experience of salvation is basic, as are familiarity with Scripture and a genuine desire to win others to Christ. Readiness to participate regularly in workshops and training courses, and in practical apprenticeship and internship experiences that may or may not lead to full-orbed class teaching assignments or club directorships, for example, is an essential ingredient for workmen that need not be ashamed. And just as the ongoing daily practice of life in Christ is—nontechnically considered—the largest panoply of Christian education, so the overall calibre and condition of the church program in operation is the most comprehensive environment and content of leadership training. What is worth doing is worth doing well is supremely pertinent to the most important work in the world, that commissioned by the Lord Himself—to make disciples who become ambassadors.

Conclusion

Professor E. S. Gaustad of the University of California at Riverside sees a bleak future if "national and personal life, religion and education" have no "fruitful interaction"; our society will be "technically proficient but spiritually vacant" . . . our nation will have "abundant knowledge about means but little wisdom regarding ends." By and large the West has lost the mass concept that formerly determined our life, namely, that a supernatural God is man's Creator, Redeemer, and Judge, and whose revelation is alone able to inject personal hope in the midst of a doomed and dying world. Without this lodestar of conviction, modern secular man stumbles in intellectual and moral darkness. There are those who think that Christianity has run its course. Not so, for the fact of the risen Christ will not be shaken. Faith abides for the future and will become sight; hope will become reality, love—passing over into eternity itself—will continue forever.

Although the Church of Christ will always be a minority "called out of the world," it can, if it will, take and hold the critical ideological initiative to capture the hearts and minds, wills and consciences, and bodies, too, of people everywhere. In a Way-defying universe the task of Christ's emissaries in and through the Church is to define and demonstrate the abiding tenets of the Christian world-and-life view. Preaching against assorted sins, of which there have always been many, is not enough; daily practicing the sonship to God, the indwelling reality of the Holy Spirit and demonstrating the life of which Christ is the prototype is something else. In the midst of genetic manipulation of man, we need to know and see what re-made humanity is in truth.

Current theological and biblical study is increasingly impatient, even put off, by compromised and shortcut approaches to solving man's spiritual, moral, and societal problems. In this last quadrant of the twentieth century we will increasingly push aside the one-time preoccupation with demythologizing and existentialism to personally examine the reality of God and His claims and promises. Confronted as modern man is by global atheism, by the choking tentacles of materialistic secularism, and by matter-of-fact assignment of omnicompetence to empirical science, the future task of Christian education, in and outside of the Church, may well become the most strategic responsibility it has ever faced to win the human mind and will for Christian theism. At stake is every neighbor soul in the universe; to fully exploit this challenge only wholeness of love from and toward God dare constrain us.

CHAPTER IV

The Liturgical Imperative of Religious Education

John H. Westerhoff III

To contemplate the future is to reflect on both visions and priorities. On occasion, therefore, I have asked someone: what would you do if, in the future of your dreams, you could do only one thing? Of course, most people are not anxious to respond. What dreamer wants to anticipate limits? Nevertheless I have decided to play the game.

I have a clear vision for the future of religious education. It is described in broad strokes in my 1976 book *Will Our Children Have Faith?* But in this chapter I will limit myself to the one essential and central aspect of that vision and in detail both discuss and recommend it to the church as my priority for the future of religious education.

Education To Be Christian

For too long we have associated education with schooling—religious education with church schooling and catechesis with catechetics. Before I can say anything else about the future, I must dispel this limited and limiting understanding. As long as we think of schooling as the context for religious education and instruction (teaching and learning) as the means, we will be unable to envision or plan an educational ministry adequate for the church's life and ministry in the 1980's.

In the future, religious education will need to be understood as any deliberate (intentional and reasoned), systematic (integrated and holistic), and sustained (continuous and overtime) effort within a community of faith which enables both individuals and the community to live under the judgment and inspiration of the gospel to the end that God's will is done and God's community (kingdom) comes.

Obviously a host of diverse efforts are necessary to reach and sustain such a goal. Still one aspect of church life stands out as both prior and central to the church's ministry and mission: namely, its rites and rituals.

Cultic Life of the Christian Community

"By their rites you will know them" is more than mere rhetoric. We humans cannot live without rituals. We cannot do without worship. We simply cannot exist without an understanding of the world and established correct ways of living. And such understandings and ways (faith) necessarily are expressed collectively in symbolic acts (rites and rituals). Through "rites of community" the church sustains and transmits its faith. Through "rites of change" the church enables persons to make transitions in their faith pilgrimage and life cycle.

No aspect of community life is more important than its rites and rituals. This is not hyperbole. We humans are made for ritual and in turn our rituals make us. No culture is complete without common beliefs and ceremonial practices. A community's understandings and ways are invariably objectified in ceremonial observances. No people have ever been discovered who fail to share some articulated set of beliefs about the world and their place in it. And nowhere is there a people who fail to engage in ritual acts to sustain and transmit their beliefs. Faith and ritual cannot be separated. Recall that when the prophets sensed that the people had forsaken their faith they attacked their rituals. But when the people were in despair over their faith and lost in the struggles of the soul they called them to return to their rituals.

Worship is at the center of the church's life. The word orthodoxy means right ritual. The rites and rituals of a Christian faith community are the most significant aspects of its life. That is why ritual is so difficult to change. We all know that it is easier and more acceptable to preach a radical sermon than it is to change the order of worship. That is true because the structure of our rituals provide us with a means for ordering and reordering our lives. Our rituals telescope all our understandings and ways, unite us in community, give meaning and purpose to our lives and provide us with purposes, guides and goals for living. That explains why, when our understandings and ways of life change, we are apt first to cease participating in the rituals that once inspired and sustained us. It also explains why our first need, after casting aside old rituals, is to birth new ones.

Changes in our understandings and ways result in changes in our ritual life. And changes in our rituals produce significant changes in our understandings and ways. That is why some people want the church's rituals to change and others do not. Every reform movement in the history of the church has involved liturgical change. Indeed the most revolutionary changes in Christian history have resulted from liturgical reform. Reformations and ritual renewal go hand in hand. The cultic life of a faith community, therefore, needs to become the focus of religious education and the priority of our educational ministry.

Educational Dimensions of Ritual

Now when I say that ritual must be central to our educational ministry I do not want to give the impression that I believe worship is education or that education is everything in the life of the church. But I do want to contend that education is an essential part of every aspect of the church's life—especially its worship.

In regard to ritual, our educational ministry has two dimensions. First, we need to consider the role liturgy plays in the life of our faith community and especially what beliefs are being sustained and transmitted. In most cases we have been mindless about the ordering of our ritual life. We rarely ask what is being learned by those who participate in our rituals. And we almost never place our rituals under the judgment and inspiration of the gospel to see how well they enable us to live, individually and corporately, to the ends that God's will is done and God's community comes. To engage the community of faith in such radical reflective actions is primarily an educational task.

Second, we seem to forget—or neglect—to provide opportunities for persons and the community to prepare for meaningful participation in the community's rites and rituals. Religious educators need to assume responsibility for this necessary preparation. Too often, even when we do engage in some sort of educational efforts related to our rituals, they have little or no relationship to each other. It is as if liturgists and educators never speak to one another.

A few months ago a group of my students and I conducted a research project on rites of initiation in Protestant religious communities. Through the anthropological method of participant-observation we studied a large number of diverse groups. When we completed our work, it was necessary to develop a typology for rites of initiation: namely, rites of institutional incorporation and rites of faith commitment. In spite of the rhetoric by all groups that faith was their goal and the presence of significant faith content in the rituals, we concluded that most mainline Protestant churches were primarily concerned with institutional incorporation and survival.

For example: confirmation classes were typically called membership classes. Preparation dealt primarily with denominational polity, history and practice; financial support of the church; participation in congregational life and attendance at worship. The ritual itself typically contained two sorts of questions. The first dealt with matters of faith and the second with institutional commitment. In most every case we discovered that the leader of the ritual behaved in preferential ways toward the latter. For example, one set of field notes after another disclosed that after quickly asking the faith questions, the minister paused, looked the candidates in the eyes, spoke more slowly and listened carefully for their reply. Is there any doubt which questions were considered most important? Further, when adults and parents were asked if they would be upset if their children decided against confirmation, they typically answered "yes." But when asked why, everyone replied, in one way or another, that their children would be lost as church members. Not one parent in two hundred interviews expressed concern for their children's souls or faith.

Because we have failed to understand the importance of unity between our rituals and educational endeavors, we have both improperly prepared persons for meaningful participation in the faith community's ceremonial life and continued to encourage persons to mindlessly participate in rituals which often are antithetical to Christian faith. Only when we grasp the centrality of ritual for the church's life and educational ministry will the educational mission of the Christian church be realizable.

The Nature of the Christian Faith

At the heart of the Christian faith is a story. Indeed, at the heart of every community's life is a story—a story which explains its understanding of the world, the place of persons in that world and the ways of life they are to pursue. One essential role of ritual is to communicate the community's story in ways that help it become internalized and owned. Religious education also shares a concern for making *the* story *our* story. Too often, however, very different stories are being communicated and learned in the church. The educator's responsibility is to help the community get its story straight.

The Christian story is a story of God's mighty deeds—God's actions in history. It is a story about a vision. In the beginning God has a vision of a world at one with itself, a world of peace, justice, freedom, equity, whole community, and the well-being of all. It is the world God intends.

God creates persons in "his" (her) image as historic actors whom God intends to have live in and for God's vision. But God also grants us the freedom to say yes or no to "his" vision. And so the plot thickens. We humans are more interested in our visions than God's vision. We create systems (principalities and powers) which benefit some of us but not all of us. As a result of our own selfish actions we become isolated from nature, ourselves, each other, and God.

But God persists in seeking after us. God calls a community, our foreparents, into being to witness to "his" vision. And God takes the side of those who are either kept outside or oppressed by the systems we humans create. God, biased to the hurt and the have-nots, acts on their behalf that "his" vision might be realized. God liberates the slaves in Egypt, patiently pulls them toward "his" vision, and establishes a covenant with them to live as "his" visionary community. Still it does not work. As soon as we humans begin to receive the blessings of God's vision we act to keep these blessings for ourselves alone. God continues to raise up prophets to remind us of God's intentions for "his" world and a faithful remnant keeps the story of God's vision alive.

Nevertheless, it is as if we are in bondage to the social forces, to political, economic, and social systems we built. Over and over again some individuals catch a glimpse of God's vision and commit their lives to its realization. Yet that vision still remains a lost dream. So God makes a decision. God acts again, enters our human condition, becomes incarnate in Jesus of Nazareth, the story teller, doer of deeds, healer of hurts, advocate of the outsider, liberator of the oppressed. Through Jesus the good news is announced: God's community has come. In the absurdity and foolishness of the cross God acts to liberate us from bondage to the principalities and powers. Nothing—no social, political, or economic power can hold us any longer, and so on Easter morning the disciples behold the dawn of God's coming community.

Yet the dawn of hope is not yet the high noon of God's community come on earth. Darkness still covers much of the land, people are still oppressed, wars continue, poverty and hunger prevails, injustice is perpetuated, and the mass of humanity is still marginal to God's promise. Even many of us who claim the name Christian continue to frustrate God's vision and live as if we do not understand the implications of its message. We bless our individualism and competition. We say this is the best of all possible worlds. And we justify our way of life.

God calls prophets forth to remind us of "his" vision and the radical demands it places on our lives. The gospel itself judges and inspires us. Here and there some live according to God's will and for God's coming community. And each week the community of faith gathers to celebrate its hope, to point to the signs of God's coming community, to announce that we are liberated from the principalities and powers, and to stimulate us to act with God for "his" vision.

The church is the bearer of that story. And when that story becomes *our* story we will know what the name Christian means. Ritual is concerned that the story be known and owned. Education is concerned that this story be understood and applied. We had better agree on the story.

Liturgy: The Work of God's Visionary People

Rituals can be dangerous. They can act to bless and sustain the way things are in the world. They can induct people into accepting society as it is. Indeed that is what every culture asks of its religious institutions and expects of its rites and rituals. But the God of the Christian faith asks something very different. God calls the church to be a community of cultural change. Our rituals are to aid us in critically judging the world, to provide us with visions of the world God intends and to motivate us to live in God's world as strangers and pilgrims. Our rituals in the Christian church are meant to induct us into a provolutionary community which is willing to die for the transformation of the world into the community of God. The Christian faith is truly radical. It demands that we seek justice for all who are marginal, become advocates of the have-nots, liberate the oppressed, and seek the well-being of all.

Too often our ritual life provides an escape from the world and a support for the status quo. Too often our educational programs socialize us to both accept these rituals as good and to uncritically participate in them. Liturgy—the work of God's visionary people—properly unites ritual and social action. Our rituals must, if they are to be Christian, equip and motivate persons and the community to act in the world for social change. Likewise our social actions must be informed and inspired by Christian understandings and ways communicated and sustained through meaningful rituals. That is why theology is prior to both education and ritual.

The church needs to understand that the Christian faith is biased to all those who are marginal and oppressed. God is the one who sets people free. The gospel announces the good news of liberation. We have hope amidst the evil of life because we have a memory of God's past actions and visions of God's intentions. Salvation is a social event in the present, an engagement with history, not an escape from history. We humans are responsible for joining God in the shaping of history.

But we cannot be Christian alone. Community and corporate identity with all God's children are not optional. Our created corporate selfhood places us in an essential relationship with all others. We cannot be in community with God unless we identify with and seek the good of all people especially those outside the system, the have-nots of the world.

Religious education and the shape of our liturgies have placed an emphasis on individual growth and social change through a gradual evolutionary process. Optimistic about the improvement of the race and social progress, we have placed our emphasis on nurture, thereby neglecting human nature and the gospel's call to repentance.

We can no longer surrender to the illusion that child nurture in and of itself can or will rekindle the fire of Christian faith in persons or the church. We have expected too much of nurture and its supporting rituals which at their very best make possible institutional incorporation. We can nurture and ritually induct persons into institutional religion, but not into mature Christian faith. The Christian faith by its very nature demands conversion. We cannot gradually educate persons through instruction in schools to be Christian. Nor can we gradually lead persons to

Christian understandings and ways through our contemporary rituals.

Neither the pietist who has no commitment to the struggle for justice and righteousness in the world of institutional life nor the social activist who has no personal commitment to Christ are truly converted into mature Christian faith. True conversion—authentic Christian life—is personal and social life lived on behalf of God's will in the political, social, and economic world.

The converted life is a provolutionary existence over against the status quo and committed to a vision of God's coming community of liberation, justice, peace, whole community, and the well-being of all people. We cannot be nurtured into such a life—not in this world. Every culture strives to socialize persons to live in harmony with life as it is. But God calls "his" people to be signs of Shalom, the vanguard of God's coming community, a community of cultural change. To reach the conviction that such counter-cultural life is our Christian vocation and to be enabled to live such a corporate existence in-but-not-of-the-world necessitates reformed rituals and new corresponding forms of education.

The church is best understood as a creation of God, a community of corporate social agents called to bear witness, individually and corporately, in word and deed, to God's intentions for human life. The church is called to be a radical community for others, a counter-cultural community biased to and acting with God on behalf of the oppressed, hurt, poor, have-nots of the world. The church can never exist for itself. It is never an end, only a means. Its mission, its end, is to be a community where Christian faith is proclaimed, experienced, understood, lived, and acted upon. The unification of liturgy and education is essential if the church is to be the community of faith God intends.

Too often we have led persons through our ritual life to lives of mere inwardness or personal piety, thus blessing the existing social, political, and economic orders regardless of the injustices they may perpetuate. The covenant of God's people with the Lord of history entails responsibility for the total character of society. To restrict religion to the immediate relation between an individual and God or to an individual's relationship with another individual is pietism. Pietism is a turning from the God of the Christian faith, a denial of the sovereignty of God over the whole of life and thus a heresy. To neglect the social world and institutional life is to deny the sovereignty of God over the whole of life; it is to practice an idolatry, for it confines God to individual existence and limits Christian life to individual behavior thereby leaving the world to the principalities and powers.

God intends that the church be a witnessing community of faith, a converted pilgrim people living under the judgment and inspiration of the gospel to the end that God's will is done and God's community comes. Unless our rituals support and encourage such radical existence they are not Christian. The educational ministry of the church needs to provide a way for the community to examine, judge and reform its rituals in the light of this faith. To ignore this responsibility is to be ignorant of the central role ritual plays in the lives of people and their communities. We can engage in all sorts of educational efforts but our ritual life will always be more significant and influential in determining our understandings and ways. Needless to say, that awareness should help us to shape our educational ministries in the 1980's. Any strategy for religious education in the future must unite liturgy and education and must make ritual the focus of our theological concerns.

Rites of Community

The first of two major types of rituals important for religious education are those which I call "rites of community" (sometimes referred to as rites of solidarity or intensification). These rites follow the calendar (weekly or yearly) and both serve to create solidarity and to reinforce the community's commitment to shared understandings and ways. Through participation in these rituals the community both sustains and transmits its faith. Rites of community in the Christian church follow the seasons of Advent, Christmas, Epiphany, Lent, Easter, Pentecost, and Kingdomtide. Through these weekly rituals the faith community dramatizes its story and thereby telescopes its understandings and ways.

Historically the Christian church has structured its weekly liturgy in particular ways intended to express its faith and to order the lives of its people. This liturgy has assumed many forms, but the one I find most consistent with Christian faith begins when the people of God gather in the name of the Lord to hear God's Word as contained in the scriptures and to be confronted by its meaning and contemporary application.

The liturgy continues when, as a proper response to God's word, we affirm the community's historic declaration of faith saying "We believe . . ." and thereby reestablish our identity. Having affirmed the Christian faith as ours, we naturally turn to the condition of God's world and express our concerns through prayers of intercession. Prayers of confession follow because on other occasions we have heard God's word; we have affirmed our faith and prayed for the world, but we have not lived accordingly. We need to confess our sins of omission and commission; we need to receive God's word of acceptance. Only then can we boldly strive once again to make a proper offering—a commitment to live in the world as the people of God.

Following this offering of our lives, we share the kiss of peace and proceed to celebrate the victory party of the people of God. Through the joyful sharing of this thanksgiving feast we gather the strength and courage to go forth into the world as disciples and apostles of the crucified and risen Christ. To that end we are commissioned and blessed.

That is one historic understanding of the faith as dramatized in ritual. Others are, of course, possible. Religious educators should encourage and enable the church to examine its rites of community, to discern what understandings they perpetuate and what ways of life they encourage.

All too rarely is that done. Once I recall teaching a senior high class on worship. They learned that the offering was a symbolic, communal act in response to the gospel of the people's intentions and commitments for life in the world. They said the offering revealed a people's understanding of what it meant to live the Christian life—to pick up our crosses and follow after Christ, our

Lord. They then concluded that the church's money offering once each year for racial justice, did not meet all the criteria of a Christian offering. They suggested asking the congregation to place on the altar an offering of money and a signed fair housing pledge card. That would have been a significant Christian offering, but the congregation was unwilling to participate in such an act. Perhaps the adults did not share their understanding of the Christian faith or perhaps the adults did not realize the importance of ritual for expressing, sustaining, and transmitting faith. In any case, the estrangement of education and liturgy made both ineffective.

In the future we should make preparation for participation in worship the focus of our educational ministry. I recommend that we consider the hour before the Sunday liturgy as an opportunity to do so. Have the congregation gather (all ages) in the fellowship hall before the morning liturgy. Remember it is a great mistake to separate children from full participation in the ritual life of the church. When worship is not intergenerational we miss one of the most important and significant opportunities for Christian education.

In this context new persons can be welcomed, a sense of community restored and the needs of persons ministered to. New hymns, responses, and the like can be learned and the lectionary can provide the basis for significant preparation for worship.

For example, the scripture lessons to be read in church can be the content for a variety of intergenerational learning experiences. Following this hour of educational preparation the people can process together into the nave for the morning ritual.

But much more needs to be done if we are to help persons prepare for meaningful participation in our rites of community. For too long we have engaged in education which has mirrored the emphasis in psychology and pedagogy on cognition and thinking. We have, it seems, turned faith into a way of knowing. Of course, knowing is important; thinking is important. In the light of the anti-intellectualism which has infected the church, this cannot be overemphasized. But thinking alone is not enough.

I would like to defend the contention that we are essentially agents—historic actors whose lives are best understood as a gestalt of thinking, feeling, and willing. We are created to act in the world as spiritual beings. That is why we are called to live the life of prayer—the spiritual life—or, as I prefer, daily existence lived in relationship with God through adoration, confession, petition, intercession, and thanksgiving.

Adoration, as I understand it, is focusing our lives upon the nature of God. It is the life of the dreamer which makes possible sharing God's vision for the world. Confession is the continual self-examination of our personal and social lives in the presence of God. It is living life under the judgment and inspiration of the gospel. Petition and intercession are bringing our wills into line with God's will. It is joining God in "his" community building. Thanksgiving is our active daily expression of gratitude to God for his continuing action in history. It is the celebrative awareness of God's actions in our midst on behalf of "his" coming community.

We are told by Jesus to pray without ceasing. Surely that does not mean to live on our knees uttering words to God. Prayer is rather living consciously in the presence of the God who acts in history through persons and communities to establish "his" community of love, power, and justice. It is historical life lived with a conscious awareness of God's presence. It is life so lived that our wills and God's are united in common historical reflective action. Prayer is a radical ethical activity. It is passionate social action which results from serious reflection.

If such an understanding of prayer is to prevail, if the spiritual life is to be made possible, if we are to become thinking, feeling, willing agents of God's coming kingdom, then (1) we need to recover an historical awareness; (2) we need to integrate our intuitional and intellectual modes of consciousness; and (3) we need to take seriously our volitional lives.

Numerous examples of the spiritual life in the bible support this understanding. The scriptures assume an historicist perspective. Operating from that perspective, the prophets, understanding history as the place of God's creativity, used their intuitions to hear the voice of God and their intellects to reflect on God's Word so they might act with God in history.

Moses' experience with the burning bush led him to reflect on his life and to bring to his people a vision and message of liberation. Jesus' struggle of the soul at Gethsemane led him to make a conscious decision to choose the foolishness of the cross. The awareness of Christ's presence in the breaking of the bread at Emmaus led the disciples to lives of apostleship. None of these intuitional experiences or their resulting volitional acts were purely rational or intuitional. Each represents a worldy intuitive experience which through the complementary use of the intelect led to new sorts of moral behavior. Each represents a new worldly historical consciousness of God and praxis (reflective-action) according to "his" will.

To understand persons as thinking, feeling, willing historical actors is to support the growth and development of a persons' intellectual, intuitive, and historical modes of consciousness.

Religious education requires first that we help persons regain their God-given ability to wonder and create; to dream and fantasize, imagine and envision; to sing, point, dance, and act; their natural ability for ecstacy, appreciation of the new, the marvelous, the mysterious, and for sensual and kinesthetic awareness; their God-given talent to express themselves emotionally and nonverbally.

Concern for the religious affections must once again become a central concern of church education. Participation in the arts must become an essential focus of our educational ministries, through our liturgies and church life.

We need also to focus on the development of historical awareness. That will not be easy. We live in an historical time. We have been taught our history as a meaningless collection of dates, names, and places. Few are conscious of a meaningful past and most consider the past they do recall as irrelevant to the present. As a result many are trapped in the present. Story telling needs to become a natural and central part of church life. And we must learn to tell *His* story as *our* story. No longer can we explain how the Israelites were ever in bondage in Egypt and God saved them. (Who cares?) Instead we need to use all the arts to explain how *we* were once oppressed in Egypt and how God liberated us. Our rituals must aid us.

We must once again become a history-bearing community of faith. We need to become a story-telling people who seek to communicate God's story as *our* story. Our ritual life must be judged, informed, and inspired by how well it nurtures our spiritual lives, our lives as the provolutionary people of God.

Rites of Change

The second major type of rite, important for Christian education, is what I call "rites of change" (sometimes referred to as rites of passage or transition). These rites help us to make life's changes meaningful. They aid persons and the community to reorder their lives and adjust to change. In the church, our major rites of change follow the pilgrimage of faith: baptism, first communion, confirmation, ordination, and last rites. Others such as marriage, coming of age, moving, the establishment of a home, a new job, and retirement can also speak to changes in our human condition in the light of the gospel.

Our educational ministries must take such rites and rituals seriously and like our rites of community be understood, evaluated, and when necessary reformed. Further, educators in a faith community have the special responsibility of preparing persons to participate in these rites and rituals of change.

Rites of change have three stages: separation—transition—reentry. In order to help persons change in their status or role within a community there is first a structured experience of separation from old status and roles. Next comes a structured experience of death and rebirth, a turning point or ordeal of transition and change. And last is a structured experience of both adjustment to new roles and status and reentry into the community as a new person. When this third part of the rite is complete the person has been reincorporated into the community and is established in his or her new status.

A rite of change incorporates all three of these stages and may last for quite some time. For example, the rite of marriage begins at the engagement and continues until the married couple is fully established in their home. The ritual of change, however, contains the same three stages by telescopes them into a short moment of time in an orderly, predictable, and stereotyped ceremony. Religious education needs to but a major dimension of the church's rites of change, particularly during the separation and reentry stages. Religious education should especially prepare persons to participate in the ritual which symbolically dramatizes the transition experience of each step in a person's faith pilgrimage.

In terms of our pilgrimage in Christian faith I advocate the following rites of change and their concurrent educational endeavors. Each deserves a chapter in a book, but for now let me only make a few short conversation-producing comments.

1. Baptism

Baptism dramatizes that grace of God, given prior to any human response, which fully incorporates a person into the community of faith. As such it is appropriately celebrated with the children of the faithful and their parents. To do so requires the serious preparation of the parents.

Appropriate preparation should begin early. As soon as a couple is aware that they are to be parents (by birth or adoption) they should come before the congregation to announce their anticipation, be blessed and receive the prayers of support from the community. Also at this time, Godparents (faithful members of the church) should be called forth from the congregation to aid the future parents in preparation for their child's baptism.

For the next nine months the parents, Godparents, other children, and relatives living nearby should meet for a weekly fellowship meal, family liturgy, and discussion that will prepare them spiritually for their new responsibilities. These conversations should focus on the vows which will be taken at the child's baptism, the parent's faith, and the implications of the Christian faith for family life and child rearing.

If the child should die before birth a supportive community exists. If the child is born, the parents and Godparents are prepared for the child's baptism. Also a supportive community has been formed to aid the parents to fulfill their baptismal vows. For nine months after the baptism this extended family community should continue to meet. Then each year until the child's first communion the parents, Godparents, and the child should celebrate the child's baptism day by coming before the congregation to witness to their growth in faith and their effort to share their faith with their child.

2. First Communion

Sometime before the first and third grade a baptized child and their parents may enter a six month's preparation program for first communion. This important ritual dramatizes the child's decision to participate in the ritual life of the community. Weekly intergenerational opportunities prior to the Sunday Eucharist continue the educational efforts made in prepartion for this rite of change. As a faithful participate in this weekly rite of community, children will experience belonging to the faith community, nurture their religious affections, come to know the Christian story as their story, and understand the grace of God given in the sacraments. They will witness the radical life of the Christian community and ritually share in its understandings and ways.

3. Covenant

Through the years the church has made an error in celebrating confirmation in early adolescence. At a time when youth should be encouraged to doubt and question their faith, engage in intellectual inquiry, explore alternatives, and learn to give their life away, we ask for a final commitment of faith and a declaration of intention to live the radical life of the Christian. To meet the needs of transition into adolescence or the need to belong, youth have mindlessly participated in confirmation. As a result the development of their faith has been arrested and they have been either inducted into institutional status-quo religion or graduated out of the church.

What the church needs is a new ritual for early adolescence to be celebrated on St. Thomas's Day and based upon texts from the scripture, such as Jacob wrestling with the angels. Such a rite of change would aid youth in their faith pilgrimage and usher them into a period of intellectual struggle between their faith and that of the community. Religious education needs to prepare persons for participation in this rite and provide follow-up educational experiences that are consistent with the covenant made with God and the community of faith at this rite of change.

4. Confirmation

I do not believe a person is ready for confirmation before eighteen years of age (twenty or older is better). If the church is to become a radical provolutionary community of converted disciples, confirmation must become a pivotable rite for the church's educational ministry.

During Lent each year the church should hold a series of inquiry retreats. Their purpose: to introduce young adults to the radical nature of confirmation and the ordeal of preparation. On the Sunday after Easter those who wish to become confirmands should present themselves before the congregation and announce their intentions. A sponsor of mature faith should be called from the congregation and assigned to each confirmand. During the next twelve months the confirmands and their sponsors would engage in the following:

a. Four spiritual life retreats.
b. Weekly participation in the eucharist and after each retreat a report to the congregation on their faith pilgrimage.
c. Daily private devotions and bible study.
d. Weekly gatherings for prayer, a fellowship meal, and conversations on Christian faith and life.

   e. Participation in at least one social action, social service and evangelism project.

   f. An artistic creation in drama, music, dance, or art of the Christian story to be presented to the congregation during Lent.

   g. Engagement in the study of God's intentions for the church, and the institutional church today, followed by the learning of those institutional change skills necessary for the reform of the church.

The final preparation for confirmation should take place during Holy Week. On Palm Sunday the confirmands should review the promises to be made at their confirmation and then make their final decision. On Maundy Thursday they should be dismissed before the liturgy of the Lord's Supper. At this time they should begin a period of meditation, prayer, and silence in the church. On Good Friday they should attend the services in sackcloth and ashes. On Holy Saturday they should present their artistic creations of the Christian story to the congregation.

On Easter Eve the congregation should gather in the dark of the church to prepare for Easter and pray for the confirmands. Just before midnight the confirmands, having heard the prayers and hymns of the congregation, should take a drink of milk and honey, put on white robes, and as the bells of the church ring in Easter, light their baptismal candles from the Pascal candle and process into the church singing. As they enter, the confirmands should light the candles of the congregation (the faith of the new confirmands rekindles the faith of the congregation) and present themselves for confirmation. Following their confirmation they would be the first to receive the Eucharist. For the next six months they should continue an educational program aimed at making their new life in the church meaningful.

5. Ordination

Another identity and faith crisis occurs in the late 30's and early 40's. It would seem appropriate that the church consider the ordination of all persons to their Christian vocation in the world at this time. Obviously serious preparation would have to be made for this rite, but it could be a transforming rite for persons and a reforming rite for the church as a community of change in the world.

6. Last Rites

Regretfully the church has not yet developed adequate educational programs to prepare persons for this terminal rite of change. We need to learn to celebrate the lives of the Saints. That challenge lies before us.

The Opportunity and the Challenge

It is important to realize that I wrote this article as a Protestant Christian. My examples may have seemed strange to some readers. But I hope that no reader will miss my main point in any possible disagreement with my illustrations. That point is this: Liturgy and education must be united and ritual must become the focus of our educational ministry. And both must be an expression of our provolutionary, radical Christian faith.

In any case this chapter is not an exercise in crystal-ball-gazing. I have not described the educational ministry I think will be. Rather I have described the educational ministry we need, but will probably not have unless we radically rethink and reshape our understandings of Christian faith and education. At best some Protestants and Roman Catholics have understood the importance of liturgy and education, but few have made it central to their educational ministry. That we must do.

To accomplish this end, local congregations will need to assume much more responsibility for religious education. Seminary education will need to be changed in significant ways to prepare clergy and laity for this new responsibility. And the field of religious education will need to be radically changed. I am committed to these ends. In the years ahead I plan to work for them as advocate, theoretician, and practitioner. Who will join me?

CHAPTER V

Modeling Religious Education for the Future

Gloria Durka

The major need that confronts American religious education in the immediate future is not money, nor buildings, nor power, but is, rather, the necessity for a totally new conception of the way the church should educate its members. It is true that changes have been made as challenges have arisen, but these have not affected the basic conception of religious education. The single overpowering need for the religious education we need is to rethink the purposes, the aims, and the objectives of religious education, and to devise a new structure and substance to meet those purposes. Obviously, this chapter cannot pretend to offer a final synthesis on religious education. Nevertheless, a modest attempt can be made to consider some points that are most crucial for the religious education we need.

Clearly, the failure to think seriously about educational purpose, and the reluctance to question established practices is not the monopoly of religious educators. This failure is diffused all too evenly throughout the entire educational system, and indeed throughout the entire society. The failures of the ghetto schools, for example, are in large part a reflection of the failures of American schools as a whole—to educate all people to full humanity. Religious education most especially should facilitate people's ability to live full, human lives. The "how" of this remedy will largely depend upon the way we rethink and restructure the very substance and purpose of religious education.

This chapter will be concerned with three levels of this task: the process, the places, and the persons.

THE PROCESS

There is no doubt that the profession of religious education could change radically in the next few years. The question is more one of desire or will, rather than the technical question of whether the knowledge base of professional religious education is susceptible to change.

No matter how compelling the reasons for change, though, professional religious education most certainly will not evolve automatically to a higher state of development. Serious modification will come only after a clear conception of what constitutes desirable professional education is affirmed and a deliberate strategy for implementation is enunciated. I think that at this juncture in our history, religion and science have joined to foster new ideas in the education community that could be woven into the fabric of new professional religious education.

The main thrust of the new substance of religious education must be a change in the way religious educators think about religious education problems. This means that this rapidly changing world demands a questioning, inquiring attitude and new "content" presented in new ways.

The emerging highly interactive, regenerative technological society requires something akin to mass genius, mass creativity, and lifelong learning. The world is changing at an exponential rate. If religious education is to meet the challenges wrought by changes in science, technology, communications, and social relationships, religious educators cannot rest on the answers provided in the past, but must put their trust in the processes by which new problems are met. This is so because change overtakes us so rapidly that answers, methods and skills become obsolete almost at the moment of their achievement.

This implies not only new techniques for religious education, but new goals. In this kind of world (which is already upon us) one of the goals must be to develop individuals who are open to change. Only such persons can constructively meet the perplexities of a world in which problems spawn much faster than their answers. Religious education should be geared to developing communities in which people can live more comfortably with change than with rigidity. As Carl Rogers has suggested, in the coming world the capacity to face the new appropriately will be more important than the ability to know and repeat the old.

This work is concerned with the kind of religious education we need. Such a future-oriented question is of significance not only to professional theologians, but to practitioners involved in religious education as well, because such a question is so fundamental that it cannot fail to have profound effects upon the whole educational spectrum. If the future world is to be one in which people will have discovered how to live in community, religious education must first return people to themselves; that is, it must educate the emotions, the senses, the so-called aesthetic sensitivities. This is difficult because, as Abraham Maslow pointed out, we do not know enough about the "learning of the heart" which has been neglected for so long. Yet is is a task which must be encouraged at all levels. Process theology can be helpful here since it borrows heavily from evolutionary insights as well as from theological and philosophical categories.

To formulate faith or belief in the context of an evolutionary universe is the task incumbent on philosophers and theologians today. Formulas that are separated from the revelatory action of God in persons' lives can in fact constitute a positive hindrance to revelation.

In other words, I think that what is needed is the radical attempt to work out a theological pattern for Christian faith which is in the main influenced by process philosophy. Such an attempt must use insights gleaned from the existentialist's insistence on engagement in the world and responsible decision-making, the understanding of history as involving genuine participation within specific social contexts, and the psychologist's awareness of the various depths of human experience.

Process thinkers do not merely reiterate the great traditions, nor do they simply affirm a new conception. Rather, they give more articulate development to old religious and philosophical insights hitherto neglected by the great system makers of the West, but long present in philosophy and theology, struggling for a more adequate hearing.

History proves that people cannot respond creatively to the new possibilities opening up in the historical process when their anxieties over the uncertainty of the future drive them to cling to the apparent security of the past. People cannot exercise power positively and constructively when the complacency or despair of believing that nothing can be done about the way things are seems preferable to the vulnerability that inevitably accompanies actions aimed at actualizing new possibilities for the fulfillment of human life. If people are not hopeful, they cannot be responsible.

Responsibility suggests the power people have to shape their own lives and the life of the world. People are never mere products of forces they cannot control. Indeed, not only can they make effective decisions about the utilization of new possibilities presented to them in the forward movement of history: they can also bring into being new possibilities not already present in the situation.

Christianity has always been the religion of an infinite future, and there is no way to go back to past ages supposedly more religious than the present. I think that process theology can help people realize that God is nearer than ancient people could ever have imagined. The "golden age" is not behind us, but ahead of us, but such an awareness is only possible when we take seriously the formative imagery of our contemporary experience.

Process thinkers affirm that no theology is final and that for this reason, we will have to learn to live with a plurality of theologies. None of these theologies may be perfect, and none of them has a monopoly of the truth, but each of them will be able to speak with a special clarity to some given sector of contemporary society. What will be needed in the future as well as now is to be aware of and accept pluralism in its incomprehensible and uncontrollable aspects. This will mean living with the persistent awareness of the futility of attempts to achieve an all-encompassing view of the world. Yet, I think that such tentative interpretations do not presage a future of unbelief but a future of greater belief.

Herein lies the most critical and all-embracing question we will have to face: are the institutional structures of Christianity broad enough to accommodate persons who are widely divided on the doctrinal basis of the faith and on the very meaning and purpose of the church and of religious education, or are the divisions already so deeply entrenched as to make accommodation impossible? I suggest that whatever be one's preferences for particular positions in the search for truth, all positions should be allowed to continue being rethought, for it is mainly through the plurality of formulations that we can arrive at what is relevant, adequate, and true to human experience.

Process theologians are engaged in such a task and are aware that such attempts are necessarily essays on reconception. They make no pretense to being conclusive or exhaustive. Their response to pluralism is an appropriate one—it is not one of avoidance or of accommodation. Rather, it is one of helping persons to better recognize, understand, and affirm the infinite variety of theological symbolizations available in life, while at the same time proposing a model which may more appropriately mediate reality to many contemporary Christians.

THE PLACE

Any consideration of the future of religious education must begin with the effectiveness of schools, for it is within that framework that most of those engaged in religious education operate, and from which most religious education settings are derived. Yet it is glaringly obvious that schools are not enough to effect the kinds of changes that will be necessary in the immediate future if religious education is to deliver on its promise to improve the overall quality of life in society. This point has already been made in the American bishops' pastoral letter, *To Teach As Jesus Did* (1972). Would that we take their exhortation seriously.

A good example in point can be learned from "public" education. The brief history of education programs like Head Start has already proven indisputably that such programs cannot compensate for the environmental differences that children bring to school. Any stimulus to learning must be intensely consistent over a *continuous* period of time. Head Start demonstrated that a temporary stimulus cannot counteract the continuing effect of the environment.

The principle behind Head Start was that children who were not up to a desired level of readiness could continue to progress on their own, once they achieved the desired level of readiness. Their failure supports the theory of religious education suggested by Gabriel Moran in *Religious Body* who sees effective religious education as that in which the whole community educates the whole community to make free and responsible choices which reach out towards the whole world. Indeed, the total environment has a continuing effect not only on the rate of learning but also on the "absolute" level of performance. The process of education is no longer perceived solely as that which transpires between student and teacher. Formal schooling provides for only a part of human development, while family life, community agencies of all sorts, and the general cultural and aesthetic milieu contribute to individual growth.

When a society is undergoing rapid change, such as ours presently is, it is wise to reexamine all of its institutions, especially its educational institutions, for those institutions must "fit" with the broader society. The task of all educational institutions is to bring people toward adult maturity in *that* society, not just any society, and they should be fitted to that task.

What this seems to indicate is that, even though it is probably not very popular to say so, most of the problems religious educators face in their programs are problems of total environment, not of schooling in the narrow or formal sense. What is needed is a new type of religious education that incorporates a wide variety of ideas. This notion is especially important with regard to the adolescent. I do not mean to suggest that schools play the most important part in the adolescent experience. On the contrary, what is already apparent is that far too many young people, from a wide variety of socio-economic backgrounds, find the confinement to a student role to be an inadequate preparation for life. And this will be even more apparent in the next few years. What is essential is not to minimize schooling, but rather to provide institutions that give adolescents a much broader role than that of a student.

Here again, a brief overview of the history of education in the United States quickly reveals that schooling often creates the myth that nothing is as important as academic performance. I think religious educators should have no trouble admitting there is more to life than good grades. In 1903 John Dewey addressed the First Annual meeting of the Religious Education Association and called for the educators to realize that education should provide the child with the means to grow into adulthood. He stressed the obligation of the adult community to accept the fact that what children need most of all is to be supported by a sense of security and significance. Such a sense is crucial to promote growth into responsible adulthood. I would hope that in the next few years we will have created youth environments which contain schooling but are not limited to it—environments which would more adequately sponsor the transition into adulthood.

Along these lines one can suggest at least some things which should happen in the more immediate future if we would take seriously the realities of the society we live in when we set about to design religious education programs. For example, religious education, both formal and informal, should begin at earlier and earlier ages and should extend into all ages. There should be a dramatic increase in nonschool education. All possible resources of the community should be used to educate people. In many instances the schools should be replaced by a diffused learning environment involving churches, home, libraries, parks, public buildings, resource centers, guidance centers, and the like. More and more, the family unit must recognize that it is basically an educational unit. Parents should begin consciously designing their homes as life-long learning environments.

In the case of the poor, I should like to see even more than the above. I see the need for religious education programs to reach out directly to poor families in their own homes. Teams of well-trained religious educators would be needed for neighborhood blocks and low-rent housing projects. Such programs would be more successful than school-centered programs because the family and the home would be educated and improved together.

Schools have always been based on the concept that teachers do possess a certain expertise, and this establishes the basis for the student-teacher relationship. While there is much to be said about teachers as facilitators and learners themselves, it must be realized that teachers and students are not partners adrift on the sea of ignorance. In an effort to facilitate dialogue and "community," teachers of religion often assume a false posture of "camaraderie" which makes them susceptible to ridicule. This danger could be avoided if religious educators themselves would be more critical of what they do. The professionals and paraprofessionals must become critics of all aspects of education. I would hope that professional religious educators would move to overcome the shortcomings of the profession by developing standards for on-going criticism of the religious educational practices. Indeed, I suggest that not only is criticism desirable on the part of religious educators; it is part of their trust.

It seems to me that we must rethink and reconvince ourselves of the importance of self-criticism. Self-criticism is necessary because it enables us to exercise some control over the future. But self-criticism is difficult, particularly in religious education, because so few have attempted to do so in any scientific manner, and because so much of what passes for criticism is merely the projection of one's own biases. We judge lightly and know only superficially. We tend to think that we judge correctly when we have only begun to take the first step in that direction.

Since all forms of institutional life we find in the church and in society are open to change, we should be able to construe the critical approach as both process and product. A climate of criticism could then be created that would be self-reinforcing and would affect the entire field of religious education. Further, such a climate would encourage the critical integrity of the church.

This should not be construed as a blanket endorsement of competency-based teacher education programs which presume to reduce teaching to a set of performances that can be imitated by relatively untrained people such as paraprofessionals. Competency-based teacher education as it appears to be conceived and practiced is quite the opposite of the professional approach to teaching, that is, the education of teachers who are conceptualizers, who understand their tasks in a broad, theoretical framework. What is being advocated here is that religious educators who profess to be teachers must be professionally qualified.

Professionalism means that practice has been elevated above the status of an art. Therefore, teachers must possess a body of knowledge about teaching that surpasses their own experience; they must know at an advanced level what they are to teach, and they must have developed inquiring spirits about both what they know and how they practice. Competence in a field of endeavor means, clearly, the developed ability to describe, explore, explain, and reflect upon the data which identify a field. This is essential to the attainment of the objectives implicit in the various models used to pursue an end.

Of course, it can be admitted that teachers can come to teach very effectively without ever being consciously aware of what they are doing. One can teach extremely well without ever having taken any specific courses in the methods of teaching, but this is so accidental as to be unpredictable. On the other hand, if teachers are to comprehend the grounds for their work in order to improve the relationship between act and intention, and realize consistency and adequacy in their teaching, they must study the models on which their actions or methods are based. We can and do absorb methods in all sorts of ways. But until we have studied the theories on which they are based, those methods are never really ours. We are theirs, and we do what unexamined habits direct us to do.

The churches must find a better way of using the experience and expertise of all the teachers, administrators, specialists and paraprofessionals who engage in religious education at all levels. No other field has such a large number of practitioners, and no other field has such a need to capitalize on the insights of its participants. Then perhaps programs could move in the direction of separating management and education so that they would approach a "program which provides for religious education" rather than remain a "religious education program." To facilitate such a move, there should be a unit known as educational advisors attached to diocesan and/or regional offices, whose function it would be to stimulate innovation and encourage the use of the most advanced educational practices at every level of education.

Most educators already agree that the most important single source of new substances for professional education is the social sciences. Much has been done to identify conditions favoring major advances in the social sciences (psychology, economics, politics, mathematical statistics, sociology, philosophy, and anthropology). Scores of major achievements or breakthroughs have been made since 1900 that have provided consistent avenues to understanding and effecting various human behaviors. Some of these examples with pertinence to education include Weber's sociology of bureaucracy, culture, and values, which is the basis for organizational theory; Freud, Jung, and Adler's psychoanalysis and depth psychology; Bridgman's operational definitions, which define abstract concepts in terms of concrete steps; and Rapoport's conflict theory and variable sum games.

Valuable knowledge more directly pertinent for teacher educators has also been contributed by a number of recent researchers. Bloom's monumental review of almost one thousand studies of selected human characteristics has surfaced the tremendous importance of early education. The significance of his work has been reflected in the interest in nursery school and kindergarten education, and in a revival of concern for the quality of primary education. Guilford's work on the structure of the intellect has resulted in the idea that learning is the discovery of information, and not merely the formation of associations. Suppes's research on principles of learning utilizing advanced computer technology has already opened up new worlds for teacher educators. Clearly, such research indicates that a knowledge base that will significantly change teacher education in the future can be established.

I would hope that in the immediate future religious education theorists would take the findings of the social scientists seriously and incorporate the insights gleaned from these findings into their own work. James Michael Lee has been the first religious education theorist to seriously advocate an approach based on the social sciences, and he has contributed much to the discussion. But much more work is needed along these lines. Needless to say, this will call for a reappropriation of efforts and resources, but the results will be well worth it. For too long have religious educational discussions been carried on in isolation from the larger educational community.

THE PERSONS

The last point to be raised here is a brief but pivotal one. It is germane to any consideration of the religious education we need, and it can be said to be tied in to the whole question of liberation. It is the issue of women in religious education.

Since it is a more difficult and lengthy process to transform institutions than it is to change ideas, the full impact of liberation theology has not yet been felt. Yet the problem of power and liberation is perhaps the most important question that the churches have faced since the Reformation. There is considerable evidence that it is being ignored precisely because the implications are too staggering to be realistically confronted. I suggest that this is especially true in the area of religious education.

In her presidential address delivered to the members of the Association of Professors and Researchers in Religious Education in 1974, Iris V. Cully traced the recent history of women in religious education in the United States. An obvious conclusion from her work is that women have yet a long way to go before they will enjoy equal status and opportunity with men in positions of leadership and power.

For too long women's role in religious education has been confined to "instruction in the faith." Women were not perceived as real educators until quite recently. Because women were entrusted with instructing the children in the doctrines and practices of the faith, religious education became associated with women and children. All too frequently the result was that the only qualification necessary to be considered a religious educator was the fact that one was a woman—or more precisely, especially in volunteer programs, a woman with time on her hands. This fact has been compounded by yet another—until very recently, the field of religious education has not been regarded as academically credible or worthy of pursuit as a field of endeavor by very many male members of the church.

I see two tasks before women today if we are to disavow ourselves of this myth.

1. The need to professionalize ourselves to new heights of excellence and competence.
2. The need to work for a new power base within the institutional church.

First, the need for professionalization. Doing more of the same harder is not likely to provide the breakthrough now needed. New concepts of religious education programs are demanded, as are new policies, arrangements of resources, and above all a new relationship of women to men in the churches, and of the churches to the community, family, and neighborhood. Part of this problem is tied into a larger philosophical one which has to do with the regard in which religious education is held right within the church community. What I mean is that religious education as it is presently conceived by many church-related groups is the height of anti-intellectualism. It is because of this that I believe one of the major problems facing religious education is the prevalence of a nonreligious analytic and research orientation toward improving the quality of religious education. So, I suggest that women religious educators especially must examine their beliefs about knowledge and their approaches to the fixation of belief. In many instances the epistemology of religious education is laden with mysticism, romance, religious fervor, and unexamined tradition. Here the obligation of professional self-criticism on the part of women cannot be emphasized enough.

Most women religious educators have been taught to accommodate themselves to the system, not to improve it. If the critical approach became a part of their preparation, religious educators could result who would consciously try to improve the system. This would involve construing the critical approach as both process and product. That is, the preparation programs would not only equip the students with requisite skills and knowledge, but they would also deliberately seek to disabuse them of myths, errors, mistakes, and inadequacies. A climate of criticism would result that would be self-reinforcing and would affect the entire profession. I am convinced that if women religious educators are to deliver on their promise to the church and society it will have to be through qualified and vastly improved professional preparation.

Second, we must work for a new power base within the church. I would agree with those who point out that if the *human* meaning of liberation is to be realized, it must finally be directed toward the emergence of an interdependent human community that has regard for the legitimate interests and aspirations of *all* people. Yet, in the short run, the crucial issue is that women who have previously played only a marginal role in the Christian church should now be liberated from their stereotype image and called to new levels of responsibility.

There is a clear axiom of modern life that those with power do not voluntarily surrender it. Women religious educators must form groups that can exercise power and work from some kind of power base, with all of the temptations and abuses to which they thereby become liable. And this because the affirmation of values or principles is of little avail. What counts is *full* and constant participation in the structures of power where *concrete decisions* are made daily. But I would hope that women would not succumb to the temptations of liberation theology which regard action more important than thought or reflection. I would suggest that reflection of the highest order is necessary to effect praxis. As David Tracy points out in his *A Blessed Rage for Order,* praxis is the critical relationship between theory and practice whereby each is dialectically influenced and transformed by the other. Otherwise, the result is sterile activism.

Women need to strengthen their place in the fields which have traditionally been open to them and should explore areas which have been off limits for them. More women should engage in scholarly research in theology and biblical studies as well as in religious education. They should hold diocesan and parish posts in which they will be responsible for decision making and policy setting. Too long has meekness gone under the guise of service. And they must be qualified. This means that more and more women should pursue higher studies and enter into rigorous training programs which will prepare them for the variety of possibilities available in the emerging area of religious education.

Women should join and engage in public discourse on educational and theological issues, and they should hold membership and leadership roles in professional societies.

Impatience may be in order, but if so, it should be clearly differentiated from an anti-institutionalism that is much better at destroying than at building. To be sure, there is an aching gap between rhetoric and reality. However, what is needed is systematic change that is connected with the larger organization. Basic changes must come also in the area of ecclesiastical structure even though the full realization of this step will be a long and painful process. But I would hope that the above remarks would underscore the fact that such a step is a necessary one if women we are to answer the invitation to effect the religious education we need.

AN AFFIRMATION

I have suggested earlier that religious education must overcome its frequent tendency toward anti-intellectualism. But it must be realized that continued and rigorous inquiry does not limit access to truth to any channel or method. It does not depend for assurance upon subjection to any dogma or item of doctrine. As John Dewey pointed out in *A Common Faith,* the method of intelligence is open and public. The doctrinal method is limited and private. The perspectives presented here do not maintain that knowledge is now or soon will be available in the final form necessary for achieving the religious education we need. It is not. What is available, however, is enough to give us confidence in recognizing the kind of work that is needed to progress toward such a goal. It is suggested that such a search will view religious education as a dynamic reality always subject to growth and development. It does, however, lack the absolute security which blind adherence to practice and theories can provide, but this is no loss. Instead, it creates a dynamic and realistic concept of the options in which accidental failure does not mean irreparable loss. It gives confidence to our creative abilities and makes us more truly the living image of the Creator.

The issues most vitally affecting the field of religious education are now being raised not in terms of its weakness, but in terms of its strength; not in relation to its ultimate limits, but in view of its new possibilities.

All the forms of institutional life we find in the church are open to change. There is no structure, no practice, no principle, so sacred, so absolute, so righteous that is above alteration, revision, or criticism. As religious educators, we must be ready to react to new realities in history by discarding even our most cherished ideas and by accepting new ones, later to be sacrificed again. This calls for a willingness to reinstitutionalize the forms of religious education based on a conscious theological recognition of what its purpose is.

Part of the difficulty religious educators at all levels experience is due to the fact that the institution they have the responsibility of defining, sustaining, and transmitting is in a serious state of flux. In particular, the church has no predictions to make, no program and clearcut prescriptions for the future of humanity in this world which could relieve it of the anguish of planning the future. But this absence of certainty need not be a terrible burden; instead, it can be an opportunity for exciting possibilities.

One fact is immediately apparent: even though the task of reassessing and revamping the whole area of religious education appears to be an overwhelming one, our real alternatives do exist now. The possibilities for the future are already with us. We can already see what the characteristics of future life in the United States will include: increasing significance of complex organizations, increasing depersonalization, increasing power of technology, increasing infantilism of youth, and increasing societal heterogeneity. These characteristics will generate more and more alienation between the persons and society, particularly if little or nothing is done to change the religious educational system.

Ours is the responsibility of conserving, transmitting, rectifying, and expanding the heritage of values we have received that those who come after us may receive it more solid and secure, more widely accessible and more generously shared than we have received it.

Obviously, the ideas presented in this article could be seen by many to present a terse analysis of the situation. I would be the first to agree that the issues are enormously complex and that the ideas presented here are in no sense adequate descriptions or assessments of this complexity. They are at best only attempts to join the discussion which is even now enjoying a new beginning. Perhaps, though, these ideas will serve to stimulate others to consider further the implications of these suggestions for the future of religious education. But of one thing I am convinced—there is little time for delay. I share George B. Leonard's opinion that the future guarantees no kindness to those who, in the name of "reasonableness" or "practicality," fail to make the larger proposals.

In view of all this, it seems to me that in redefining, reconceptualizing, and restructuring the field to effect the kind of religious education we need, our worst error would lie in dreaming too small.

CHAPTER VI

Toward a New Era: A Blueprint for Positive Action

James Michael Lee

At the very center of the church stands religious education.

The church cannot fulfill its divine or human mission without religious education.

If there is no religious education, there is no Christian church.

Such statements reflecting the centrality and indispensability of religious education in the church are clearly implied in the scriptures. The bible says that in his final commission to his apostles, Jesus told them what he expected them to do as a church, as a believing and hoping and loving community. Only two things did Jesus specifically wish the church to do: to engage in the sacramental ministry, and to teach religion (Mt. 28:16-20).

Despite the supreme importance which Jesus placed on religious education, the church by and large has not taken its founder too seriously in this matter. This is scandalous, but it is also true. Instead of standing at the very center of the work of the church, religious education has typically been relegated to the periphery. Religious education has seldom received a truly significant share of the church's personal, financial, or scholarly resources. Protestant denominations usually content themselves with a one-hour-a-week Sunday School program generally staffed by well-meaning but untrained teachers. American Catholics have erected a massive school system; yet the percentage of personal or financial attention typically allotted to the school's religion program in systematically integrating religion with the rest of the curriculum, has been relatively negligible. Furthermore, the CCD program by and large is only weakly financed.

Perhaps this unhappy situation is coming to an end, at least in the Catholic sector of Christianity. In the 1960's and 1970's, religious education increasingly commanded more and more of the church's attention. Parishes began to establish their own comprehensive nonschool religious education programs, schools started to hire professionally-prepared religion teachers, Catholic institutions of higher learning inaugurated graduate programs specifically designed to prepare religious education professionals, and a few scholarly books were published in the field.

If it is really true that a new day is dawning for religious education, then it is imperative for all of us to make sure that religious education is pointed in the proper direction else a premature and fiery sunset ensue. Therefore, it is incumbent upon us to put all assumptions to the test, to critically examine everything we have done and are doing, and to start afresh in formulating goals and objectives. Unless we take these steps we run the great danger of misdirecting our energies, our resources, our talents, and most precious of all, our vision. What I intend to do in this chapter is to reconsider virtually everything we have done and are doing in religious education. Everything must be put to that great Christian test of "*ex fructibus eorum*," namely, that the character and worth of a reality is known by its fruits (Mt. 7:20).

My purpose in this chapter is not to go into depth or to explore any one point in detail. Space is too limited for an undertaking of this scope. Rather, I will succinctly offer suggestions and recommendations which empirical research and personal experience have shown to be of probable profit for a new and a more dynamic religious education. This essay is but one chapter of a book and hence its necessary limitation in size makes it an unsuitable vehicle for any complete presentation of a program for the total reform/renewal of religious education. Therefore I will restrict myself to certain selected concepts and proposals. Though many of my comments are relevant also to Protestant religious education, I am directing my statements primarily to the Catholic sector, again for reasons of space. In a later book I plan to expand on this chapter, treating the points I make here in greater detail and offering additional considerations.

As I observe in the "Prologomenon" to *The Shape of Religious Instruction,* any educational enterprise worthy of the name provides three basic services: instruction, administration, and guidance. Because instruction is the heart and the *raison d'être* of religious education, the bulk of this chapter will be devoted to religion teaching.

SOME BASIC GUIDELINES

Empirical research findings (objectively verified data), as well as personal experience (subjectively, and to a limited extent, objectively verified data), when combined with a Christian vision, suggest certain operational principles or guidelines which I firmly believe should undergird all future religious education activities. Guidelines are highly useful for religious educators because they indicate fruitful starting points from which to inaugurate religious education programs and also provide important criteria for the continuous and continuing evaluation of all their phases and aspects. In this section I will briefly touch on some of the more important guidelines for the religious education we need.

Religious education in the future must first and foremost be religious. It is a common observation that at present many religion lessons comprise insufficient or watered-down religion. One principal source of dissatisfaction on the part of learners of all ages is that the religion programs are not religious enough. Religion programs today are not infrequently one of the last places where a Christian can learn and live his religion. This unfortunate state of affairs might possibly reflect the current condition of the Catholic church in America. Many persons of deep and sensitive religious convictions are increasingly finding that the Catholic church is not religious enough because it is de-emphasizing its primary sacramental and salvific function, concentrating instead on primarily political and social issues while still embracing a legalistic spirit which is more asphyxiating than life-giving.

Religious education in the coming age should be for all Catholics of every age and circumstance. There is a certain *grande hauteur* currently in vogue in some circles which claims that Christianity is a religion for adults, and that therefore religious education programs for children and early adolescents should be discontinued. Such a pompous and arrogant stance has no place in a religion whose founder delighted in children (Mk. 10:16), who told those who would follow him that their spirit should be like that of little children (Lk. 18:17), and who died for all persons, young and old, of every era and clime (2 Cor. 5:15). A truly Christian religious education does not disinherit any individual or group from its activities or benefits; rather, it shapes and fashions itself according to the age and other developmental conditions which characterize each learner.

Religious education of the future should become family-centered. Potentially the most successful and comprehensive religious education program is that which is rooted in the family. Life is lived at its deepest and most personal level in a family setting, a fact which holds true even for families which are fragmented or unhappy. The research data resoundingly indicate that a person's deeper value and attitude structure is established in the first six years of life, a span typically lived in a family milieu. Authentic family-centered religious education is religious education for each member of the family specifically targeted to his or her own personal, existential level. Any so-called child-centered or youth-centered family education which involves parents or other live-in relatives simply as vehicles for the religious education of the child or youth is sham family-centered religious education. The only authentic family-centered religious education is one which involves the total family qua family. Family-centered religious education is the most natural, the most pervasive, the most personalistic, and the most effective of all forms of religious education. Family-centered religious education is most fruitfully done in a family setting, not in an institutional milieu.

In the future, a careful distinction must be made between religious education and religious schooling. Religious education should not and cannot be equated with religious schooling. The goal of religious schooling is to provide the learner with a religious education. Religious schooling, whether conducted in a Catholic school or in a CCD setting, is only as successful as the religious education outcomes it facilitates. Under certain circumstances and with certain learners, other church or nonchurch agencies provide a more appropriate and more effective religious education than does religious schooling.

If the future of Catholic schooling is to be made tenable, it must fully reorient itself with respect to religious education processes and objectives.

A Catholic school exists primarily to provide the learner with a religious education more enriched than is likely to be obtained elsewhere. Thus the basic criterion upon which to judge the merits of a Catholic school is the quality of religious education it yields, as measured by gains in desired religiously-oriented behaviors of a cognitive, affective, and lifestyle sort. This criterion in no way negates the importance of a top-quality academic program in the language arts, history, mathematics, and so forth. Because the Catholic school is proximately and ultimately an agency for religious education, any conflict between it and various forms of nonschool religious education programs can only flow either from an incorrect conception of the complementary roles of school and nonschool programs or from defective implementation of one or both of these.

Religious education in the future should be intertwined with the work of the whole parish. Total-parish religious education is a very worthwhile endeavor. ("Parish" here can mean a local community of Christians organized on any one of a number of axes, such as on a geographical axis or a professional axis, to name but two.) At bottom, a parish is nothing more than a certain way of mobilizing ecclesial resources in order to render more fruitful the church's basic twin task of the sacramental ministry and religious education. Religious education is the responsibility and the work of the whole parish. Conversely, the parish as a parish is a religious education activity. School and nonschool religious education programs should be plugged into the total parish life, though not to the exclusion of other kinds of nonparish religious education enterprises. Each parish should have a formalized religious education program which encompasses and integrates the activities of both its school and nonschool arms.

In this total program, there should be one full-time, professionally-prepared coordinator, and under him full-time professionally-prepared specialists, one for each of the following areas: early childhood religious education, adolescent religious education, adult religious education, family-centered religious education, and teacher-training/leader-formation. If a parish is too small to finance this team of full-time professionals, then several parishes can pool their resources to be able to employ them. There should also be a specialist in special religious education, one who works with the mentally or physically handicapped and the emotionally disturbed of all ages. Such a professional might well serve more than one parish. The parish religious education program itself should be systematic and comprehensive, with clear, operationally-defined objectives and procedures. There is no room for a program which operates whimsically or by the seat of its pants, regardless of how such capriciousness might be defended by high-sounding but totally-misguided appeals for the Spirit to blow where he will. Experience has shown that the Spirit seems to blow most fruitfully in carefully-designed and well-implemented programs; his blowing appears to be curiously absent in ill-constructed or poorly-operated activities. Perhaps this fact tells us something about how and under what conditions the Spirit blows.

At the diocesan level, religious education should hold pride of place together with the sacramental ministry. If the care of souls is indeed the supreme law governing every diocese, then religious education, which consists above all in the care and nourishing of souls, should assume a far greater importance in the coming decades than has heretofore been the case. Like the parish, the diocese is basically the mobilization of resources to render more fruitful the church's sacramental ministry and its religious education function. Because the goal of the diocese is religious education, and because the Catholic schools (as well as social welfare offices, and so on) are at bottom agencies for religious education, the diocesan director of religious education should be the bishop's chief diocesan administrator. Under his integrative leadership should come the directors of nonschool religious education programs, directors of school religious education programs (currently called superintendents of schools), social-welfare heads, and the like. Having the diocesan director of religious education operate as the chief administrator will help insure coordination of all the religious education activities of the diocese and will act as a safeguard in preventing diocesan agencies such as Catholic schools from straying from their basic religious education thrust and character. An organization of this kind might not have been too practicable prior to 1970 when there was a relative dearth of seasoned, professionally-prepared diocesan directors of religious education programs. Since then, however, the situation has improved to the extent that directors are becoming increasingly ready to assume their rightful role as their diocese's chief administrator. Working with the diocesan director should be deanery directors of religious education. Each deanery in the diocese should not simply have a clergyman dean; it should also have a full-time, professionally-prepared religious education dean whose task it is to coordinate and integrate the religious education programs operating in school and nonschool agencies within the deanery.

Fruitful cooperation should be one hallmark of future religious education workers. At all levels, from diocesan director all the way up to the religion teacher, these workers should work continuously and fraternally with the parish's chief religious educator (the parish priest) and with the diocese's chief religious educator (the bishop). These ecclesiastics should be involved, as appropriate, in the policy-making, planning, evaluating, and reforming operations of the religious education program. Failure to appropriately involve the bishop or the parish priest runs far deeper than failure to touch the power bases. It is fundamentally a failure in working with the persons who make an indispensable, unique, and rich sacramental as well as religious educational input into the lives of the laity. After all, a bishop or parish priest who sees his role solely or principally in terms of power is not going to produce much nourishing or enduring fruit in the religious education apostolate (or in the sacramental ministry, for that matter). When working with religious educators, bishops and parish priests should operate out of their strengths, not out of their weaknesses. It is the exceptional bishop or parish priest who is professionally-trained as a religious educator. Hence their contributions to religious education ought not to be addressed to areas outside their competence, but to areas in which their sacramental powers, grace of office, pastoral experience, and personal vision equip them to make valuable contributions to the diocesan or parish religious education program. The effective bishop or priest is one who works as a partner with the religious educator; he works with the religious educator, not on him.

If religious education of the future is to be successful it should be based on and flow out of solid empirical research and fecund theory. Empirical research ought to be ongoing and continuous both during and following instructional, administrative, and guidance activities. Without carefully-conducted scientific research studies it is impossible to assert with any degree of confidence whether the desired instructional, administrative, or guidance objectives have been attained. Catholic officials in the past and even in our own day typically have eschewed empirical research on two grounds. First, they claim that empirical research methodology is *eo ipso* incapable of assessing religious outcomes. But these same officials seem never to have entertained any hesitation in evaluating a particular religion lesson or administrative effort as "successful," "not too bad," "poor," and so on, without bothering to realize that such assessments are, in fact, gross empirical measurements of the very outcomes they stoutly contend more refined instruments are unable to attain. Second, it appears that these officials have feared that empirical research might well uncover defects and deficiencies they would like to conceal from parishioners, parents, and learners. Such a closed attitude seems strange in a church which has always stressed careful and earnest examination of conscience and truthful confession. Valid empirical data are an absolute necessity if the church is to provide the religious education we need. The church of the future cannot afford, nor indeed could it ever afford, a religious education based on untested assumptions, on well-meaning but unverified hunches, and often on erroneous inferences in place of those based on hard evidence derived from empirical research. Empirical research should be primarily of the investigative, processive, and heuristic variety, not merely by the superficial "cash payoff" type which appears to be favored by some ecclesiastical officials.

Complementing and fructifying empirical research is theory. Empirical data form the basic building blocks of a successful religious education program. But in and of themselves the building blocks are useless and indeed without sense. It is theory which indicates how these indispensable building blocks can be advantageously employed, how they make sense. In religious education, theory has three primary functions: to explain educational practice, to verify the effectiveness of the practice, and to predict or generate new practices. A theory is an extraordinarily useful and practical thing; it tells a religious educator what to do and, in broad strokes, how to do it. There is nothing else which performs these services. A theory is characterized by its consistency and its system-acity. Any so-called "eclectic theory" is as vacuous and as useless as those who say they subscribe to it. Present day religious education in the United States (and in Europe as well) is rather sterile and unproductive for two main reasons: it lacks the requisite empirical data, and it has no guiding theory. Few religious educators, for example, have any comprehensive, well-thought-out, empirically-based theory of the facilitation of learning.

If future religious education is to be successful, then it will have to be grounded in a better metatheory than that which "guides" it today.

The metatheory which has "guided" religious education for so long is both useless and inappropriate. This metatheory, namely, the theological approach to religious education, claims that religious education is a branch of theology; that is to say, religious education receives its goals as well as its practices from theology. Such a position is patently absurd. Theology is as inappropriate and inadequate to dictate or generate instructional decisions as it is to dictate engineering decisions or to generate dental decisions. Religious education is not theology; it is religious education. The goals of religious education are drawn from religion and not from theology. The practices of religious education are drawn from the field of education, not from the science of theology. Religious education is not a handmaid of theology. Religious education is intimately related to theology (as well as to psychology, sociology, and so forth) but it is a field of work and a field of study which is autonomous from theology. To be "related to" is far different from being "identical to." First-rate theologians seldom have difficulty with this notion as it is virtually self-evident. The only persons who are troubled with this conceptualization seem to be fifth-rate theologians who could never make it in theology and so have drifted into religious education hoping to find there a safe port for their mediocre theological skills. If religious education in the future is to become effective, it is absolutely imperative that it adopt a social-science approach or metatheory and shed the outdated theological approach. The social-science approach is not antitheological. Quite the contrary. The social-science approach liberates theology from a bondage and an attachment it never sought, freeing it to fruitfully work within religious education in a manner appropriate to its own methodology and goals.

If there is any one basic guideline which is the most important and the most necessary for the successful future of religious education, it is this: religious education in all its aspects should become thoroughly professionalized. Professionalization enables virtually all the problems besetting the field to be resolved.

Professionalization is the aim in religious education as both a field of study and a field of work. Professionalization means an identity for the field. It means that empirical research of the finest calibre is pursued. It means that all activities flow from theory and return to enrich it. It means that teachers and administrators in religious education programs are properly trained both before service and continuously throughout service. It means full-year graduate-school preparation-programs of distinction. It means research-based curricula. It means constant focusing on the dynamics of instructional practice. It means autonomy for the field. In short, professionalism is the only way in which religious education of the future can be truly and fully effective.

INSTRUCTION

In the rest of this chapter, I will offer in condensed form many concepts and proposals which I believe should undergird religious education in the future. It is my earnest wish that teachers, administrators, and guidance personnel working in religious education programs will expand my ideas and apply them to their own situations. The future is in our hands—it will be what we make it. It is my hope that the future which we will make in religious education will be along the lines I am suggesting in this chapter.

What I say in the remaining pages applies to both school and nonschool religious education programs. Basically the same principles operate and are effective in school as well as in nonschool milieux. Teaching, for example, is teaching, and the setting in which it is done does not fundamentally alter the principles of successfully facilitating desired behavior.

Organizational Considerations

A hard-nosed reassessment should be made about the advisability of compulsory religious instruction at the elementary and secondary school levels. In effect, compulsory religious instruction is not so much compulsory instruction as it is compulsory attendance. It might well be that compulsory attendance is necessary to insure that Catholic children and youth learn the basic elements of their religion. But then again, it might be that compulsory attendance alienates more individuals from religion than it attracts to it. Religion is essentially a free commitment on the part of a person; from this perspective it can be legitimately argued that compulsory attendance is detrimental to the healthy development and nurture of this freedom. It is quite possible that voluntary family-centered religious instruction is more effective in attaining religious instruction goals than is compulsory religious instruction in a school or a CCD setting. Sophisticated experimental undertakings which compare the outcomes of compulsory to voluntary programs are necessary before this issue can be resolved with the requisite degree of confidence.

If, in the future, ability grouping and/or achievement grouping will continue to be used in elementary and secondary religious instruction programs, then it should not be done on the basis of either the learner's intelligence quotient (IQ) or his grade level. Rather it should be done on the combined basis of his religion quotient (RQ) and his religious achievement (RA), to coin two terms. IQ simply indicates a person's mental ability, while RQ indicates his ability specifically with respect to religious values. Instruments such as the Allport-Vernon-Lindzey Study of Values give us some data related to RQ. The learner's grade level only suggests what the learner has achieved as an average in all his subjects; sometimes it only means that he is of a particular age and has not missed an excessive number of classes in the preceding grade. His religious achievement score (RA), on the other hand, tells us the degree to which he has mastered the cognitive, affective, and lifestyle aspects of Catholicism. Because RQ and RA scores have such a wide range of applicability within the church, it is surely not too much to ask bishops and other ecclesiastical officials to enthusiastically sponsor research to develop adequate RQ and RA instruments.

The present lockstep pattern of religious instruction situated in Catholic schools and in CCD enterprises is at variance with almost everything the research has disclosed about learning. Learning is not determined by age or grade level alone. Learning is a highly individualized thing, and takes place at different rates in different learners. Yet we insist on putting learners into a lockstep system of fixed age-grade levels. Advancement to the next higher grade-level, oddly enough, is not determined by mastering the desired goals established for the previous grade; rather it is determined by a 60 percent or better mastery of the goals. It is vital that in the future the goals of the total religious instruction program in both the Catholic school and the CCD will be carefully established, and then translated into performance terms. As soon as the learner masters one set of cognitive, affective or lifestyle objectives, he should then advance at his own rate to the next one. For some learners, this can be done in a shorter-than-average period of time; other learners will take the average amount of time; for still other learners, a longer period of time will be needed. If time is a critical factor, then the objectives for the faster group can be enriched while those for the slower learners can be reduced in both quantity and depth.

This proposal has the added advantage of eliminating the prevalent and questionable system of marks. Because the affective and lifestyle dimensions of religion tend to be tied closely to subjectivity and personal encounter, many teachers and learners believe that marks tend to impede rather than promote the objectives of the religion program. (There is a significant difference between scores such as RQ and RA on the one hand, and marks for lessons, units, and courses on the other hand. RQ and RA scores are generalized and diagnostic, while marks are particularized, evaluative, and often punitive.) The learner does not receive marks in a program consisting of performance-based, mastery-level outcomes; he keeps on working until he has attained the desired objective to a specified level of mastery and then he proceeds to the next higher objective. In this way there are no marks, because every attainment is 100 percent. No prior evaluative assessments are made, though the learner does receive helpful feedback from the teacher and from his workmates on how he is progressing.

To accelerate the pace of improvement in religious instruction, diocesan as well as local directors should inaugurate experimental learning environments, experimental schools, experimental lessons, experimental curricula, and experimental teaching procedures. In this way progress in religious instruction will be promoted in a systematic, research-based fashion. During certain periods of its history, religious instruction suffered from a famine in innovative ideas. At other times the field was surfeited with all sorts of pioneering suggestions, some of which seemed promising and others absurd. A planned program of experimental pilot programs or pilot procedures will serve to separate the productive innovations from those whose popular appeal far exceeds their effectiveness. Planned, regularized programs of experimentation insert the growing edge right into the very structure of the diocesan or local religious instruction enterprise. It is crucial to underscore the necessity of pilot experimental programs being research-based. Unless solid empirical research undergirds these experimental programs and procedures, there is no way of ascertaining with any satisfactory degree of confidence how effective the experimental programs are as compared with those already in use.

The Curriculum

The curriculum for religious instruction lessons and courses must have religion as its substantive content. While this might seem obvious, nonetheless there have been not a few religious instruction programs whose curricula have centered around how to get along with people, social ethics, value clarification, literature, and the like. This does not imply that the religion curriculum should be devoid of enhancing social skills, value-clarification abilities, and so forth. What it does imply is that these and other areas are brought into the curriculum only to the extent that they relate to and foster the attainment of religious outcomes.

The religion curriculum of the future should revolve around the teaching of Christian doctrine. However, it is of paramount importance to note that Christine doctrine is not, nor can it ever be simply limited to the cognitive content of Christianity. Such a stricture would be a cruel twisting and distortion of everything

Jesus stood for and taught. Christian doctrine is an operational-ized pattern of life. Christian doctrine in its authentic form is Christian living. Christian doctrine is a lifestyle. This lifestyle, this pattern of conduct, contains many important and necessary cognitive and affective contents. The emphasis in the religion curriculum of the future, then, must be on lifestyle outcomes, the education of persons who will live a saintly life. This represents a reversal of the restrictive and asphyxiating cognitive stress championed, curiously enough, both by the conservative and the liberal wings within Catholicism. *Les extrêmes se touchent.* The goal of religious instruction in the future ought not so much to be the production of Christian thinkers as of Christian doers. The development of Christian thinkers should remain the task of Christian graduate schools.

CCD courses by and large have been a failure. This is not only one of the findings in the Greeley-Rossi investigation; it is also an observation made by many professional religious educators and church officials. I suspect that one of the principal reasons accounting for the relative lack of success of the CCD lies in the fact that its curriculum is mainly cognitive in cast. A cognitive curriculum is bound to run aground in any program operated for children and youth on a one-hour-once-a-week basis. If such an organizational pattern is to be continued for the CCD (and I do not advocate that it should), then the curriculum should be changed so that affective content is made its primary axis. Over the time span of the course, affective content will be retained and operationalized by the learners to a far greater extent than will cognitive content. Affective content also tends to be more intimately linked to lifestyle than does cognitive content. In an affectively-oriented curriculum, appropriate cognitive content should definitely be introduced—in a way that it is inserted into the overall affective framework rather than alongside of it. Such cognitive content will be retained and operationalized by the learners to a greater extent than is true in cases where the curriculum is essentially cognitive in character and thrust.

Religious curricula today tend to stress product content. In the future this situation should be reversed so that process content becomes the principal emphasis. (An example of product content is knowledge of certain Christian precepts; process content would be the ability to reason to these precepts or the act of living them out in one's daily existence.) Christianity is far more a process than a product. Process content, when learned, is retained and used more often than is production content. Unfortunately, religion teachers and religion textbooks typically tend to emphasize product content and neglect process content because of a lack of understanding and appreciation of the nature and potency of process content.

The objectives of future religion curricula should be stated in behavioral, performance terms. The objectives of many present and past religion curricula are more ceremonial than useful. They are filled with pious, overblown rhetoric which deters, not advances, the very outcomes which they profess to stipulate. Typical stated objectives such as "to grow in love for God" or "to really understand the consequences of sin" are vague and amorphous. How does the teacher (or learner) know when growth in love for God has been achieved? What indications are there that the learner "really" understands the consequences of sin? A curriculum, if it is to be teachable, should specify which behaviors are involved in growing in love for God. It should spell out the behaviors which constitute a "real" understanding of the consequences of sin. These behaviors should be expressed in observable performance terms, namely, that level of performance the learner must demonstrate to himself and to the teacher to indicate that he has indeed learned the behavior involved. (By behavior is meant, of course, cognitive behavior, affective behavior, and lifestyle behavior. A behavior is anything which a person does, either exteriorly or interiorly. In order to be able to infer that a particular learning has taken place, the behavior said to correlate with this learning must be expressed in a manner that can be observed.)

The curriculum of the future should have its starting point in the learner. All learning takes place according to the learner, Thomas

Aquinas once observed; modern psychology has amply confirmed this dictum of the patron of Christian education. Almost all contempoary religious instruction curricula available today start at some point other than with the learner: the bible, cognitive doctrine, the liturgy, and so forth. Such curricula are doomed from the start; they can never be effective no matter how well they are done or no matter what publicity they receive. To start with the learner is not to water down doctrine, is not to supersede the bible, is not to minimize the liturgy. It is to recognize that learning is a psychological process and not a logical one. It is to recognize that the learner learns according to the rules of his personality and not according to the logical rules of doctrine or of the bible or of liturgy. It is to affirm the indisputable fact that the learner acquires substantive and structural content according to the dynamics of his abilities and needs, and not according to the structure of doctrine or of the bible or of liturgy. To affirm that learning only takes place according to the mode of the learner is not to state an instructional disadvantage; on the contrary, it is to state a supreme advantage which insures that learning will never become depersonalized or static or irrelevant. A curriculum which really starts with the learner where he is does not embody such self-defeating subterfuges as "adapting the subject matter to the student" (translation: "sugar coating the material so that the student will be cajoled into learning something he does not want to learn").

No religious instruction curriculum in the future should be constructed solely by one group of persons such as, for example, a curriculum committee or a group of textbook writers. The curriculum should be an incarnation of the living church, an expression of the entire body of the communion of saints. Therefore the religious instruction curriculum of the future should be drawn up by a group of persons whose membership incorporates both the main strands of the People of God and the principal actors in the pedagogical dynamic (namely, the learners, the teachers, and in the case of younger individuals, the parents). A committee made up of representatives of these groups should compose the broad outlines of the curriculum. This document should then be refined and cast into teachable form by a committee of curriculum experts, that is, by persons who hold a doctorate in curriculum construction and who specialize in devising curricula. Learners, teachers, and parents should play an important role in preparing the curriculum and in modifying it to meet local needs. If Christian doctrine were indeed cognitive, a case, albeit a weak one, could be made for leaving the construction of the religion curriculum entirely in the hands of theological or other specialists. But since Christian doctrine is Christian living, then the only adequate and authentic religious instruction curriculum is that composed by the living members of the church, by Christians in the process of living Christianly.

While the curriculum is far broader and richer than a textbook, nonetheless in many future religious instruction lessons the textbook will continue to play an important role. Unfortunately, in the contemporary Catholic sector textbooks are seldom authored by persons with training in both curriculum construction and religious education. In some instances, the only competence which seems to be required to write a religion textbook series is the possession of a typewriter. Textbook publishers, eager to make a quick dollar, are usually more interested in sales than in quality. This regrettable situation should be remedied. In the future a textbook series should be planned by the People of God and written, as I suggest in the preceding paragraph, by professionally trained curriculum specialists. It should then be carefully piloted in representative field-test situations. Based on the results of these field tests, the curriculum should be revised and piloted once again. As a consequence of this fivefold process of planning, writing, research-based testing, rewriting and retesting, it takes five to seven years to issue a well-constructed and adequately piloted textbook series. Once the textbook series is released, professionally-trained specialists from the publishing company should work with diocesan supervisors of religious instruction in conducting workshops with teachers, thus providing them with the cognitive understandings and pedagogical skills requisite to optimally utilize the new textbook series.

The religion teacher of the future should not be required by the school, the pastor, diocesan director, or the bishop to use one particular set of textbooks or curricular materials and no other. Such a requirement flies in the face of the professional competence of the religion teacher and the autonomy of the religious education field. Only the individual religion teacher, working closely with the learners, the parents when appropriate, and his colleagues is competent to judge which textbook or set of curricular materials has the greatest potential effectiveness with this group of learners in this time and place. In his role of diocesan shepherd, the bishop has the obligation to see to it that what is taught in religion lessons is responsive to the teachings of the church. Yet this charge can be exercised legitimately only in a highly circumscribed and restricted way, since it is too easy to confuse personal theological preference or individual idiosyncrasies with that corpus of living doctrine and morals which should be both preserved and developed.

The religion curriculum of the future should make provision for the expressive arts. Man is flesh as well as spirit, and the expressive arts enable the spirit to be joined to the flesh in a beautiful and self-fulfilling manner.

The Teaching Act

One of the most formidable obstacles currently blocking the path to optimally effective religious instruction is the age-old propensity of religious educationists to spookify the teaching of religion. Spookification means that the religious instruction act is posited to be an ethereal, mysterious, nonterrestrial affair which is fundamentally beyond the regular workings of nature. Thus it is claimed that although the literature teacher, the science teacher, and the art teacher do indeed facilitate the learning of literature, science, and art, the religion teacher does not facilitate the learning of religion. It is none other than the Holy Spirit himself, it is alleged, who, operating in a mysterious and unfathomable manner, facilitates religious learning. We have here, quite obviously, not simply what I have for many years termed the "zap theory of grace," but the "zap theory of learning." But the empirical research data, to say nothing of common sense, clearly repudiate such a spooky explanation of religion teaching and religion learning. All the data suggest that religion is learned in basically the same manner as other topics or life goals. The Holy Spirit seems to operate within and according to the world which he has made and which he suffuses with his creative, renewing presence. The key to effective religion teaching, plainly and simply, is the possession of both an adequate theory of teaching and the skills necessary to facilitate learning. One of the first steps in improving the quality of religion teaching is to despookify the all too prevalent misconception of what religion teaching is and how it takes place.

Effective religious instruction has been seriously hampered by a faulty notion of the nature of teaching. Religious educationists like Johannes Hofinger, Josef Jungmann, Alfonso Nebreda and others of their persuasion have described religion teaching as "heralding the Good News," "proclaiming the Christian message," or "announcing God's word." Now, all this is not teaching—it is preaching. What is relevant for teaching is not the preaching model but the teaching model. The preaching model is founded on transmission, whereas the teaching model proceeds from the broader base of the facilitation of learning. Transmission is one of the least effective ways of teaching. To teach is to carefully architect teach-ful environments. To teach is to so structure the learning situation that the probability of successfully facilitating the desired goals is maximized to the fullest possible degree. Teaching is not a happening. A happening occurs by chance. Teaching, on the other hand, is a carefully planned and structured set of conditions which enhance learning. Until the religion teacher acquires this conceptualization of the nature of teaching, as well as the pedagogical skills necessary to implement it, his instructional activities will fall short of the level or the consistency of success for which he strives.

Effective religion teaching comes about basically from the pedagogical competence of the teacher, and not primarily from other factors such as the teacher's personal holiness or the Holy Spirit. Religion teaching, like the confection of the sacraments, does not occur *ex opere operantis*. The personal holiness of the religion teacher is not an accurate or adequate predictor of his success as a religion teacher. St. Teresa of Avila is reported to have once remarked: "Don't give me a holy spiritual advisor; give me a competent one." This has pointed and powerful implications for the religion teacher.

Religious instruction in the future should take to heart the cardinal dictum that all learning takes place according to the learner. Hence the effective religion teacher, like the effective curriculum builder, must start with the learner at the learner's personal developmental level. If the religion teacher wishes to successfully facilitate desired instructional outcomes, he really has no choice other than to start with the learner where the learner is. To start with subject-matter content is not to start with the learner where he is. Subject-matter content should be fashioned according to the learner, and not vice-versa. Subject-matter content was made for the learner, not the learner for the subject matter. In religion lessons the learner is at once the point of departure and the constant axis. This is not to de-religionize or to de-doctrinalize the religion lesson; it is to make religion and doctrine become incarnate in the lives of the learners. What is needed for the future, then, is a change in the psychological environment of the instructional situation. The lesson ought never to be teacher-centered but instead, learner-centered: learner-centered in objectives, learner-centered in pedagogical transactions, and learner-centered in evaluation.

The key to successful instructional practice in the future is to focus on concrete, observable behaviors. In the final analysis, this is all the teacher has to work from: concrete observable behaviors of the learner and himself. The rest is inference. And inference is never as certain or as immediate as behavior. The teacher, therefore, should constantly monitor his own pedagogical behavior in terms of the consequences it has on the learner's performance. Teaching is, after all, simply a series or a chain of antecedent-consequent behaviors. Focus on pedagogical behavior, on behavioral interactions in the instructional situation should therefore constitute the major portion of the religion teacher's preservice and inservice training.

If the monitoring of pedagogical behavior is ever to attain meaning and generalizability, it must be inserted into theory. Now the appropriate theory for improvement of instruction is not learning theory but teaching theory. Learning theory is event theory; it explains and predicts why and how an event occurs. Teaching theory is praxiological theory; it explains and predicts the why and the how of making a desired event occur. As I detail in *The Flow of Religious Instruction,* religious instruction has been hampered down through the centuries by so-called teaching "theories" which are inappropriate or even downright ridiculous. Among these pseudotheories are the dedication "theory," which holds that it is principally the dedication of the religion teacher which brings about learning; the blow "theory" (derived from Jn. 3:8), which claims that learning is not brought about by the teacher but by the Holy Spirit who blows where he wills; and the witness "theory," which alleges that learning takes place primarily because of the Christian witness of the teacher. These pseudotheories are sterile because they fail to suggest specific pedagogical practices to the teacher (what particular procedures is the teacher to employ to let the Spirit blow where he wills?) and because they do not explain why learning takes place in one situation but not in another (how does the teacher's dedication account for the variations in learning?). In contrast to these bogus "theories," teaching theory explains, verifies, and predicts effective teaching on the basis of the arrangement of all four major variables present in the pedagogical dynamic: the learner, the teacher, the subject-matter content, and the environment. Teaching is conceptualized in this theory to be the deliberative structuring of these four variables so as to facilitate the desired learning outcome.

It follows from what I have just written that the most effective teaching strategy is the structured learning situation strategy

(SLS). Whereas the old transmission or preaching strategy revolves around just two of the four principal variables in the-teaching-learning act (the teacher and the subject-matter content), the SLS strategy fashions all four variables into a situation which is optimally conducive to learning. The potency of the SLS strategy derives, therefore, from the fact that it utilizes all four major variables involved in the pedagogical act, neglecting none. Because it utilizes all four variables, the SLS is far more learner-centered and affords the learner a great deal more freedom than the old transmission strategy or any of its variants.

One of the reasons why past and present religious instruction has been and continues to be so ineffective is that it has usually revolved around second-hand experience such as that drawn from books or from the transmissionist heralding/proclaiming (read "lecturing") of the teacher. The more first-hand experience there is in the religion lesson, the more effective that lesson tends to be. Learners should be put into direct contact with real-life situations, not just with books or heraldic proclamations of the good news. Participating in experimental liturgies, working within a family context to prepare home liturgies, or accompanying a priest to a hospital where he brings the eucharist to the sick—these will teach the learner far more about the nature and spirit and workings of the liturgical God-and-man encounter than will reading about liturgy in textbooks or hearing the teacher proclaim the liturgy as a continuing mighty deed of God.

In the future, religion teachers should make wider use of student tutors. Student tutors can often provide splendid auxiliary instruction which is of signal benefit to the tutee as well as the tutor. Peer teaching frequently is an envigorating pedagogical experience and its possibilities should not be overlooked. Teaching religion often gives the tutor a definite ego-identity with religion in general and with the subject matter of the religion lesson in particular. Religion and the lesson become "my own religion" or "my own lesson."

Supervision is one of the many ways which the future offers for insuring the continuous upgrading of religious instruction. Indeed, the diocese and deanery owe it to their religion teachers to provide them with frequent high-calibre inservice assistance in the way of supervision. Supervision is not snooper-vision. It is a cooperative, nonjudgmental activity in which specialists in the structural content and the substantive content of religious instruction work with an individual teacher in the role of colleague in order to help him improve the quality of his religion lessons. If the religion teacher of the future wishes to constantly improve and sharpen his pedagogical effectiveness then it is important that he work closely with supervision specialists who can help him enhance and hone the calibre of his religion teaching. Such supervisors should not merely be experienced teachers. Experience testifies to experience; it does not necessarily or automatically testify to competence or special skill. Supervisors should be individuals who not only possess the appropriate teaching experience but even more importantly, have received their doctorate in the specialized field of supervision of religious instruction. Prior or concurrent teaching experience gives the supervisor a comradely attitude toward teachers and an inside, personal grasp of the pedagogical dynamic; the doctorate furnishes him with a high-level of supervisory skills necessary to assist teachers in the field to enhance their instructional effectiveness.

The Teacher

The teacher is the nerve center of the instructional process because it is the degree of expertness with which he exercises his skills that largely accounts for the extent to which a learner acquires the desired outcome. Since the teacher is so terribly important in determining the quality of religious instruction, it is imperative for the entire people of God, and in particular religious education administrators, to make sure that in the future both the teacher and his instructional competence will be of that calibre demanded for service in the pedagogical ministry.

In the future, prospective candidates wishing to become religion teachers should be carefully screened even prior to preservice training in college or university. The research data suggest that a higher-than-average percentage of persons enter the helping careers not so much for the sake of assisting others as for working out their own personal problems or meeting their own needs. Not a few individuals wish to become teachers because of such unconscious motivations as meeting their own dominance needs and wanting to be accepted and admired. For the welfare of both the teaching ministry and themselves, the future demands that this type of candidate be detected through a screening process and not be permitted to go on to professional preservice training. Despite the importance of such psychological screening, very few, if any, Catholic universities currently offering preservice or inservice programs for religion teachers employ a process of psychological screening.

Though it is typical both in the United States and around the world that persons seeking to teach in government-sponsored schools receive their initial preservice professional training at the undergraduate level, there is only a small handful of Catholic institutions of higher education which presently offer undergraduate preservice training for individuals wishing to become religion teachers. This is a most deplorable situation and reflects the low esteem in which the religious education ministry is held in this country today. Because persons desiring to become religion teachers must commence their preservice training at the graduate level, contemporary religious instruction faces a dual problem: many candidates become religion teachers without preservice preparation, and M.A. programs become diluted because so few of the enrollees have had prior preparation in religious education.

The history of Catholic education in the United States is a history of wasted resources. This truism applies all across the board, including religious education training programs. At the present time there is virtually no coordination or cooperation among Catholic colleges and universities preparing religious educators. What the future demands is a well-developed system of preparing religious educators for progressively higher levels of service. Catholic colleges which have a good-quality teacher training program to prepare persons for placement in government schools should also initiate a preparation program for religious educators. There should be a limited number of university-based programs offering the M.A. in religious education and a very select few (perhaps four at the most) which grant the Ph.D. in this field. These B.A., M.A., and Ph.D. programs should then operate as a carefully coordinated, well-meshed network. The B.A. program would act as discriminating candidate-feeders to the M.A. programs which, in turn, would perform a similar service to the Ph.D.-granting institutions. Conversely, the Ph.D. programs would offer enrichment services to the M.A.-granting institutions which in turn would offer enrichment services to the B.A. operations. With Catholic colleges and universities closely cooperating in the area of religious education, the entire country could become, in effect, one big campus with all the crossfertilization and excitement such a reality can provide.

Most present day preparation of religious educators is carried out at the M.A. level. That many of these programs need drastic upgrading is perhaps the most charitable thing that can be said about them. Scarcely a year passes but that at least one-well meaning priest or sister appears at a national meeting and confides to someone else: "I've just been named by the administration to head our university's religious education program, and I really don't know anything about the field. I was trained in theology (or English or mathematics). Can you give me some advice on books I should read, what kind of curriculum I should have, and so forth?"

In surveying today's M.A. programs in religious education around the country, one gets the impression that many of them were inaugurated mainly to make money for the institution. This is particularly true of summers-only programs. Colleges which do not have the resources to support a respectable M.A. program in anything suddenly erupt with a master's program in religious education. To a permanent faculty of one or two members are added "blitz professors," scholars with some reputation (usually gained in areas outside religious education) who do the best they can in a grand total of three days or a week of what is euphemistically labeled "the intensive education character of our program." The result is that many of these M.A. summer programs are traveling circuses with one or two permanent ringmasters to keep order (and collect the tuition) and with waves of incoming performers who remain on center stage in the institution for a brief appearance before hurrying to the next M.A. summer program the following week. One can hardly imagine a medical school, a law school, or even a seminary operating on such a basis. "Blitz professors" can be effectively used in a supplemental and enrichment capacity; they should never constitute the major portion of the program. Certainly no more than ten percent of the student's regular course work should be done with a "blitz professor."

A solid, high-quality, professional M.A. program in religious education is precisely that: a program in religious education and a program which is professional. The terminal objective of such a program is to produce skilled religious educators. It should not be so organized that it produces theological educators, theologians, spiritual directors, savants of the contemporary religious scene, or other desirable but inappropriate areas of service. A graduate program in religious education is not an M.A. in spiritual or personal renewal, despite what some incoming (and unscreened) students seem to think. Spiritual renewal is the purpose of retreat houses while personal renewal is a task of communities established for this purpose. A professionally-conducted master's program in religious education is not all things to all (tuition-paying) students; it is a focused professional school preparing candidates to be successful religious educators. An M.A. in religious education, therefore, should contain the following discrete but conjoined areas of study in which the prospective candidates should demonstrate competence before graduating: (1) experience or courses in religious education as a field, including its history, principles, theory, and problems; (2) cognate areas, including theology, sociology of religion, religious literature, and so forth; (3) principles of the psychology of learning; (4) principles of teaching and of the facilitation of desired behavior; (5) supervised practicum work in teaching religion. The practicum should be done in the university's teacher performance center and should feature demonstration lessons with videotape feedback, microteaching sessions, diagnostic analysis of actual religion teaching using interaction analysis instruments, and so forth.

The graduate program in religious education should be professional; it must be, for it purports to prepare its graduates to enter a profession at a designated level of competence. Hence the curriculum should not be just a series of courses loosely strung together; rather the courses should be so integrated as to form a coordinated, cohesive, and unified program. It should be the program itself which brings about this integration. If the "program" consists only in a series of uncoordinated courses, as is frequently the case in many institutions, then it is the students who are forced to make the integration. Where this situation prevails the students should be the program directors and the program directors should become the students. Integration is a function of the curriculum; it is not a task for the students.

Nor in the future should the M.A. degree be obtainable in a summers-only kind of program. The purpose of a professional program, regardless of the field, is to effect a fusion of the matriculant's personality with the demands and competencies required for the effective exercise of the skills of his chosen profession. A fusion of this kind takes time, and a five- to seven-week summer program by its very nature is simply too limited to afford a sufficient amount of time for this to occur. What happens at best is a thin layer of professional competencies laminated on top of the candidate's personality configuration instead of being thoroughly fused with it. To be a professional religious educator is not just to have an outside veneer of professional understandings and skills; to be a professional religious educator is *to be* one, to have accomplished a thorough merging of professional competencies and personality characteristics. To have a summers-only religious education preparation program is to doom the field from the very outset to nonprofessional status and competencies. There is not a single profession which prepares its practitioners in summers-only programs.

Often would-be candidates, especially priests and sisters, plead that the religious vocation shortage in their dioceses or religious institutes is so acute that they must staff teaching positions full-time and can be available only in the summers. What these men and women are really saying is that they do not regard religious education as a profession, though indeed they wish to be treated as professionals. Despite the vocation shortage, no bishop sends his priestly candidates to seminaries in the summers only, nor do sister superiors advocate summers-only novitiates. Catholic colleges and universities which conduct summers-only programs are directly and unpardonably contributing to the continuing nonprofessionalism and unprofessionalism of the field of religious education. A professional preparation program is one which is housed in a full academic-year program, supplemented (not supplanted) by summer school and other kinds of auxiliary enrichment experiences. Preservice work in the future must recognize this fact.

A professionally-oriented M.A. program in religious education can be offered only by a college or university which enjoys academic freedom. A profession is characterized by autonomy. Unless the college or university enjoys autonomy it will tend to produce mindless drones instead of professionals. Any preparation program in religious education which is under the control of the bishop (such as the so-called "Catechetical Institutes" which have sprung up in some dioceses) or which is subject to the Curia (such as "Pontifical Institutes for Catechetics" that have been established in the United States and abroad) fails to meet the criteria of professional autonomy. Indeed, it probably is true that such operations do not aim to train professionals but rather individuals whose most outstanding competency is their ability to act in reflex agreement with ecclesiastical officials. It is unfortunate that some ordinaries and some curial bureaucrats do not even yet appreciate that the welfare of the church is less effectively served by persons prone to respond in reflex-like agreement with every pronouncement than by trained professionals whose very professionalism enables them to break new ground and ransom the future.

Throughout this century papal pronouncements as well as documents from various Vatican sacred congregations have emphasized the necessity for future priests to receive training in religious instruction theory and practice during their seminary careers. While by and large professing their solidarity with Rome, nonetheless American Catholic major seminaries only in exceptional cases have a vibrant, well-developed program in this area. This situation is shocking in view of the fact that religious education in all its dimensions constitutes one of the two principal functions of a priest. It is hardly surprising, therefore, that a 1975 survey of priests in the St. Louis archdiocese reported that in terms both of proximity to their conception of the priestly ideal and in order of importance to themselves, the priests who responded ranked celebration of Mass as highest and high school religion (and secular subject) teaching as lowest. Because religious instruction is so very central in an authentic priestly ministry, the seminary curriculum of the future should have a vigorous and well-developed program in this field. Each major seminary should have on its permanent staff at least one full-time professor of religious education. This individual should have received his doctorate specifically in religious education and not in another field such as theology, church history, or philosophy. The seminary curriculum should include courses in the history and theory of religious instruction, the principles of teaching and learning; it should also have extensive practica and supervised field experiences in religious education. Practica and field experiences should be done in a wide range of religious education ministries and not be limited to a high school religion teaching setting. Because of the skill and capability of professionally-prepared laypersons to teach religion in school milieux, and because of the sacramental powers which are the unique possession of priests, it is neither fitting nor advantageous for priests to teach religion in high school. Rather, priests should engage in those aspects of religious education which are most closely conjoined to the sacramental ministry in the concrete here-and-now situation, for example, in hospital visitation, family work, and the like.

If the future is to be competently addressed, then every religion teacher, priest and sister and brother and layperson, regardless of whether he or she teaches in a school or nonschool religious education program should hold a license to teach religion. The minimum requirement for this license should be the master's degree with a major specifically in religious education. Surely if government school teachers are required to have a master's degree it is not unreasonable to expect that religion teachers also possess the M.A. degree. However, simple possession of the master's degree should not be sufficient for certification. The traditional professions of medicine and the law have their own special requirements for licensing: in addition to a professional degree from an accredited university, the applicant must sit for a test given by a nonuniversity agency expressly established to determine his competence to practice, and on the basis of the test results, to grant or withhold certification. Certification of a religion teacher should not be the prerogative of the local bishop or of the Vatican's Sacred Congregation of the Clergy as occurs in some dioceses in the United States and abroad. These officials lack the professional competence to make that kind or level of specialized judgment necessary for granting a license. Only a group formally representing the profession can properly issue a license to practice. Therefore the religious education profession should establish a licensing committee which will prepare, administer, and evaluate licensing examinations for persons seeking to become accredited religion teachers. Licensing examinations should be of both the paper-and-pencil and the performance varieties. Moreover, they should include a psychological screening profile of the applicant. The licensing committee should be drawn from a representative range of outstanding religious education theoreticians, practitioners, and administrators and should cooperate with (but not take orders from) the appropriate national committee(s) of the United States Catholic Conference. It is imperative that the licensing committee be representative—almost always in the past, national or diocesan Catholic religious education groups have rarely been catholic, consisting as they did only of members of the catechetical Establishment, an in-group characterized by its bureaucratic make-up, its traditional theological approach to religious instruction, its lack of daring, its lack of prophetic vision, and its antipathy to scholarship and research.

If religious education in the future is to become professional, if it is to become truly committed to excellence in the Lord's service, then obviously there can be no place for volunteer teachers as the core of the program. The nurturance of religious development is just as important, and indeed more important than the promotion of physical development. It is fully as hurtful for parents to send their child to a volunteer untrained religion teacher as it would be to send him to a volunteer untrained physician. We take health quite seriously; it is about time for us to begin taking religious education seriously. If a church does not have sufficient resources to hire professionally-licensed religion teachers, then such a church does not have sufficient resources to be a church. Volunteer teachers trained at the paraprofessional level can, of course, offer valuable *supplemental* help to the regular, paid, full-time staff.

In the future, the religion teacher's formal professional training should not stop when he becomes certified. New developments in religious instruction theory, new refinements in pedagogical practice, new insights in theology and biblics, new liturgical practices—all these necessitate that the religion teacher continually upgrade and enhance his professional skills. Every two years a religion teacher should be required to take relevant inservice courses. These courses should be sponsored and staffed by the diocesan central office for religious education. Since the essence of religious instruction is the actual facilitation of learning, the biennial inservice program must perforce include work in the teacher performance centers which the central office has established in key locations throughout the diocese.

The religion teacher of the future should be held accountable for the product and process outcomes ensuing from his pedagogical activity. Accountability helps the teacher keep his focus firmly fixed on the objectives of those learning experiences which he is facilitating. The parish religious education coordinator (who in the future should be in charge of both school and nonschool religious education), in cooperation with the teacher, learners, parents when applicable, parish priest, and representatives of the parish devise the broad objectives for the course. These objectives are then refined and put into operational, performance terms by the coordinator, the parish specialist in teacher training, and the teacher. Then these three professionals, assisted by a diocesan supervisor of instruction and the diocesan curriculum committee, if necessary, draw up procedures whereby adequate and continous evaluation of the course can occur. By this means the level of the teacher's instructional effectiveness can be fairly and adequately gauged. The religion teacher is accountable to the Lord for the stewardship of his own life. So also should he be held accountable to the People of God in the parish and the diocese for the stewardship entrusted to him with respect to his learners.

To him from whom much is demanded, much should be given to enable him to meet this demand. The religion teacher has many demands put on him by virtue of the importance of his mission and the background and skill needed to discharge it effectively. To attract and retain the best qualified persons, the salary and working conditions should reflect the axial importance of religious instruction. If religious instruction is to come of age in the future, then the religion teacher working in a school setting should receive a salary ten percent higher than a person of the same educational level and experience teaching in the local government school. A religion teacher working in a nonschool setting should receive a salary equivalent to one working in a school setting. The workload of religion teachers at the high school level should average three classes per day; in no instance should it exceed four, else preparation, teacher counseling, and cooperative staff work suffer seriously. CCD teachers should be drawn from the regular staff; volunteer teachers should be totally eschewed except as supplemental paraprofessionals. Teachers from school or nonschool milieux should conduct the CCD lessons and these lessons should be included in, not added on to their regular workload. The religion teachers are the crack troops of the parish and diocesan educational effort, and they should be treated accordingly.

ADMINISTRATION

Future local and diocesan administrators of religious education programs ought to be much more aware of the true nature and proper exercise of administration than appears to prevail among some of their counterparts of today. The etymology of the word "administration" reveals its authentic character—it is derived from two Latin words meaning "to minister unto." The administrator, then, ought to be the servant of the teachers, parishioners, parents, and learners. This is not only good spirituality; it is also sound administration.

Today's religious education is frequently administered on the management model. The program is headed by a boss or manager who single-handedly (sometimes with the "advice" of subordinates) directs the personnel and the program. The management model generates an adversary relationship between administrators on one side, and the teachers, guidance personnel, and staff on the opposite side. Future religious education programs should operate out of the collegial model. The program ought to be headed by a collegial group representing the various major subgroups within the entire program. In this kind of arrangement, the administrator serves (not bosses) the group by facilitating and implementing the policies set forth by the group itself. This facilitation is carried out in a helping, serving, ministerial fashion rather than after the manner of a manager. The collegial model generates a colleague-relationship in which the administrator ministers unto the group.

Power tends to corrupt and absolute power corrupts absolutely, runs the familiar saying. But clerical power corrupts clerically—that is to say, corrupts absolutely and with religious sanctions erected (often artificially) to back up this absolute power. The sustaining of a future colleagueship model will doubtless be contingent upon the establishment of a system of checks and balances to restrain any tendency on the part of the administrator(s) to covertly or overtly overturn the collegial model and subtly or openly revert to the management model. Original sin is a fact of life and even administrators who come into office with the purest collegial and ministerial intentions can be turned away from this goal by the pressures which they perceive their new administrative post imposes on them. A system of checks and balances represents an honest, aboveboard, and circumspect way of saying: "We really trust you as an administrator, but let's cut the cards just the same."

One way of introducing checks and balances into the system is to institute a provision that the major administrators of the religious education program be elected at regular intervals, say once every five years. Such a stipulation serves as an accountability review and also as a deterrent to prevent the administrator from being power-centered. Furthermore, it helps to keep his ministerial role continually before his mind. Periodic elections in no way preclude the development of a strong cadre of career religious educators or of career religious-education administrators. The 1975 Kramer survey revealed that the annual turnover rate of diocesan directors is about 25 percent. Such a situation is quite detrimental to upgrading and professionalizing religious education; it also is indicative of the low opinion which religious education occupies in the minds of those who are responsible for appointing and relieving these diocesan directors. In the future a sufficient corps of well-trained career administrators must be developed. If, in fact, a particular administrator does not work out well in terms of the quality of his service and overall effectiveness as determined by performance, then there should be an adequate number of other qualified persons to step into administrative posts.

At present the overwhelming number of diocesan and local religious education administrators (particularly directors) are priests. There is no worthy explanation to justify this situation. From the spiritual perspective, it can be argued that administration is not especially congruent with the sacramental powers unique to the priesthood. There really is no priest shortage in the United States; it is just that priests are staffing all sorts of nonpriestly jobs. From the organizational perspective, it is evident that competence and not clerical station must be the watchword in the selection and retention of administrators. Laypersons, including women religious, should in the future be able to advance to positions of top leadership in religious education—not because they are laypersons but because they are competent. The search for an administrator of a diocesan or local religious education program must be a search for a person who will do the job most effectively, not for a priest who can be found willing to undertake the responsibility or one who can be counted on not to make any waves.

As servants are accountable to those whom they serve, so too should administrators be accountable to those to whom they minister. It is an age-old tradition in the church that authority is service. This is a rich and fecund concept, not a base or sterile one. The administrator of a religious education program is one to whom authority is given by the bishop, by the People of God, and by his colleagues. His fulfillment as an administrator (and as a person whose function it is to be an administrator) will be in proportion to the degree to which he ministers and serves, a ministry and stewardship for which he must give an accounting both to God and man.

In the local or diocesan office of the future there should be a group of full-time, professionally-trained administrators whose number is large enough to minister effectively to the religious education needs of the parish, deanery, region, or diocese. No administrator can be expected single-handedly to handle every-thing by himself. Insufficient manpower tends to breed autocracy and inefficiency on the part of the person carrying the overload.

All future religious education administrators should have received that level of preservice and inservice preparation requisite to equip them for the satisfactory discharge of their ministerial obligations. For national, diocesan, and regional administrators, a doctorate specifically in the administration of religious education programs should be the minimum preservice requisite. This doctorate should not be in an allied or nonallied area such as theology, canon law, or mathematics. A doctorate in theology or in mathematics is as inappropriate for engaging in the administration of religious education as a doctorate in religious education administration is inappropriate for becoming a theology professor or a mathematician. Doctoral work should be completed prior to service as a national, diocesan, or regional administrator and not undertaken during it. Administrative service is not a training ground; it is a post which assumes adequate professional training before it is begun. It is difficult to understand why so many religious education administrators in the 1960's and even today expect their teachers and parishioners to take religious education seriously when they themselves are still doing only part-time or summer work to get their Ph.D. (or just their M.A. in some cases) in order to become qualified for the position which they are already occupying.

Before a person is admitted as a doctoral candidate in an administration of religious education program, he should be psychologically screened. Special attention should be paid to the level of dogmatism or authoritarianism which the screening instruments reveal.

The Ph.D. curriculum in the administration of religious education program should include work in the following areas: religious education as a field, including the history, the principles, the theory and the problems of religious education; the psychology of learning, of teaching, and of administration; developing and constructing religion curricula; work in vital cognate areas such as theology, religious studies, sociology of religion and so on; educational research methodology; supervision of instruction; and the administrative act. Course work in the supervision of instruction and in the administrative act should be both speculative and practical. In the practical dimension the candidate should be involved in practica where he engages in the administrative act, an act which is videotaped and subject to self- and staff-analysis using sophisticated empirical protocols. A section of the university's teacher performance center should be permanently set aside for such activities as micro-administering. Finally, the candidate should be required to spend a period of scaled internship in various administrative settings in which the university supervisor and the on-site cooperating administrator will help the candidate to further hone his administrative skills.

Inservice improvement is just as important for administrators as it is for teachers. In the future, the national office as well as groups of dioceses should conduct regular inservice courses for religious education administrators. These courses should be organized around the major areas which comprised his preservice training. Two things every administrator should do to continue his personal inservice training is to carefully monitor in a behavioral fashion his own administrative behavior and to engage in professional reading. An administrator who does not spend, on average, a minimum of from one to two hours daily in professional reading will soon become stale in his work.

Religious education in the future compared with that of today will witness a much greater and productive use of outside consultants. At the present time only a minority of diocesan administrators of religious education programs engage outside consultants. Those outside consultants who are called in typically tend to be persons who are supremely safe, who will make a few innocuous suggestions couched in that kind of ceremonial language calculated to please diocesan officials, and who shine more as banquet luminaries than as hard-nosed researchers or creative theoreticians. Consultants of this harmless genre seldom do more than discreetly proffer a suggestion or two before packing their bags and heading home. In the future, outside consultants should not be of the hit-and-run variety. They should be hired on a permanent retainer-basis and should make a definite and continuous input into the organization and operation of the diocesan religious education program. Some of these consultants should also be trained specialists in educational research so that existing weaknesses and inefficiencies are exposed and creative, future-pointed programs instituted. First-class theoreticians should also form an integral part of the consultant team, since these are the men and women who above all are capable of charting the course for the religious education we need. Outside consultants should be drawn from universities, from the national office, and from other dioceses or localities.

GUIDANCE

At the present time guidance personnel are by and large restricted to Catholic schools in which their activities are pretty much confined to counseling and lending assistance with academic records. In the future, guidance workers should serve in all sectors of the religious education enterprise and ought to function in a more diverse and organizationally-fecundating fashion.

There is no real justification for not expanding the efforts of guidance personnel to the larger religious education arena. Guidance workers are needed to work side by side with religion teachers and administrators in a total parish-centered religious education apostolate. They should be deeply involved in family-oriented religious education, in CCD work, in religious education for the mentally and physically handicapped, in early childhood and adult religious instruction programs, and in the whole spectrum of religious education. To confine guidance to a school setting is to at once adopt an imperialistic stance on the Catholic school's efficacy in the parish or diocese and to take a dim view of the real worth and validity of nonschool religious education.

Guidance today is regarded as primarily a one-to-one counseling activity. In the future, guidance should be interpreted and operationalized in a more expansive fashion. The guidance worker should come to regard himself chiefly as a person who serves as a resource specialist in human development to the entire religious education team. The guidance worker is an intimate member of this team; he is not outside it. But within the team he functions as the individual who is professionally trained and competent to offer help and to undertake projects which will enhance the personalized religious living of those to whom the entire religious education team ministers. Thus, for example, the guidance person should be deeply involved in curriculum construction and revision to insure that the curriculum encapsulates the principles and the data on human development and incorporates to an appropriate degree what used to be called "the guidance point of view." The guidance person assists teachers who wish to further humanize their lessons. He sees parents and children who might be having conflicts. In all things and in all ways he should act as an energizer for unleashing human potential, all within the context and goals of the religious education enterprise.

It all too often happens today that the guidance worker operates his own shop. Sequestered in his own school office, he carries on his activity in splendid isolation, above the academic din and battle. In the future, the guidance worker should operate in and through the entire religious education program. His work should be carefully integrated into the whole religious education program. Structurally speaking, he should be given tasks and responsibilities which deeply and intimately involve him with all the aspects of the program and with all the other members of the religious education team.

Perhaps because of personal inclination, or perhaps because of the mystique attached to his career, today's guidance worker has the definite tendency to don a symbolic beard at the slightest symptom and to try to engage in psychotherapy. If the guidance function is to be of optimal service to the religious education of the future, then he must hold such an inclination in check. Individual counseling is an important function of the guidance worker; however, as I suggested in the preceding paragraphs, it is only one among many of his activities. Further, the guidance worker is typically untrained as a counseling psychologist or as a clinical psychologist. Therefore he is not competent to function in such a capacity. To do so is to practice psychology without a license.

It should be underscored that there is no research evidence to indicate that psychotherapy, even when practiced by professionally-trained individuals, is successful. Indeed, virtually all reviews of the relevant empirical research conclude that there are no data which suggest that verbal psychotherapy is any more beneficial or effective than nonverbal psychotherapy. Time seems to be the major variable in accounting for any change occurring during verbal psychotherapy—and time is a resource available to a person whether or not he undergoes therapy. Besides, the research data indicate that the efforts of relatives, friends, and valued acquaintances have a greater salutary effect on a person than does a psychotherapist. To be sure, there is a large group of psychotherapists today who contend that in the final analysis the only thing a psychotherapist can really do effectively is to be caring toward the patient. This offers great encouragement to teachers, to administrators, and to all members of the religious education team. If the religious educator truly cares for those to whom he ministers—and most importantly, if these people perceive that the religious educator does in fact care—then psychotherapy in any of its verbal forms is unnecessary and superfluous. The ability and skill to effectively care are essential requirements for entering and engaging in the would-be profession of religious education. One key task of the guidance worker in the future should be to help religious educators to sharpen and refine their caring skills. Caring is an ability but its effective use is a skill which must be learned.

The focus of the guidance worker's activities in a religious education enterprise ought always to be on religious counseling. Personal counseling, social counseling, vocational counseling, and scholastic counseling are important in the religious education framework to the extent to which they further religious goals. It well may be that in some cases effective personal or social counseling is the most successful path to enhancing religious development. This is the decision which the professionally-trained guidance worker will have to make. However, personal, social, vocational, or scholastic counseling which has only a tenuous link to religious goals and processes should not be undertaken by the guidance worker operating in a religious education setting. There are other agencies in our society which perform these particular guidance services.

It is a documented fact that the psychology-related professions tend to attract to their ranks individuals having personal and emotional problems considerably in excess of the normal range in the population. Consequently in the future, guidance personnel should be screened much more carefully prior to their preservice preparation and before they enter the religious education field. Preservice work should include an M.A. in guidance and counseling, with a curriculum which meets the demands for certification, and at the same time integrates appropriate course work and experiences in religious education and religious guidance. No person should be allowed to become a guidance worker in the religious education enterprise unless he has this kind of M.A., unless he has been duly certified, and unless he has been screened. Ordination to the priesthood or final profession of religious vows do not automatically bestow guidance skills upon the recipient. Professional training is required of every prospective guidance worker regardless of whether that person is a layman, a priest, a brother, or a sister.

Continuing inservice work for guidance personnel should include courses in guidance and counseling theory, enhancing the counseling act, working more effectively with other members of the religious education team, and helping administrators to remain oriented to the personal dimension of their role. All but the first demand that the inservice work be conducted in a practicum with videotape facilities using appropriate instrumentation, micro-counseling situations, and other laboratory procedures. Inservice courses should typically be conducted by the diocesan office.

CONCLUSION

Perhaps some of this chapter's suggestions and recommendations for the reform/renewal of religious education might at first blush seem impractical, fanciful, and romantic. Yet surely they are no more impractical than so much of the ineffective and frivolous things currently taking place in the field. Religious education in the past and present has not been nearly as successful as it should—to put the matter in the most favorable light possible. My suggestions, flowing from sound theory, empirical research, and controlled personal reflection offer a concrete blueprint for making the religious education ministry more effective in the future. I see nothing impractical, fanciful, or romantic about this.

If and when contemporary religious education tries to shape the future, it often resorts to gimmickry in an attempt to accomplish this task. But gimmickry will not shape the future; in the long run it will block any truly effective efforts to forge that kind of future we so urgently need. If religious education is to shape its future in an authentically creative, innovative, and successful manner, then it must eschew gimmickry and embrace a comprehensive, systematic program of overall renewal generated by fruitful theory and supported by empirical research.

Professionalism remains the key to any effective hastening of the future. Professionalism is that high-level form of activity born of theory, backed by empirical research, and honed by ongoing professional training. In no way can professionalism be said to make the religious educator cold or the field impersonal. On the contrary, professionalism enhances the educator's warmth and makes him more effective. It fuses his warmth with the requirements of the educational ministry. It insures that the personal qualities of the religious educator will be used not for the gratification of his own personal needs but rather for the benefit and welfare of the persons to whom he ministers.

A thoroughgoing, comprehensive, professionalized program for the fruitful reform/renewal of religious education carries with it a high price. The price involves personal, institutional, and financial resources. Persons who complain about the high price, or who even ask what is the price should reexamine the depth and the sincerity of their commitment to the religious education ministry. No true apostle will waver at any price which might be asked, for no price is too high when one is working for the Lord. Surely we who claim to be religious educators cannot in good conscience kneel in prayer and say: "Lord, we won't pay the price."

For surely the Lord will answer quietly and in sadness: "My brothers and sisters, don't you think I'm worth it?"

Profiles of Contributors

ALFRED McBRIDE is the director of the National Catholic Educational Association's National Forum of Religious Educators. A priest of the Canons Regular of Prémontre, Father McBride took his bachelor's degree in philosophy from St. Norbert's College, and his master's and doctor's degree in religious education from The Catholic University of America. He has served as a teacher in St. Norbert High School (Wis.), and as assistant professor of religious education at The Catholic University of America. Father McBride has also worked as a parish priest in Wisconsin, as well as novice master in St. Norbert Abbey. He holds memberships in the Religious Educational Association and the National Catholic Educational Association. Dr. McBride's books include *Homiletics for the New Liturgy* (Bruce, 1964), *Catechetics, a Theology of Proclamation* (Bruce, 1965), *A Short Course on the Bible* (Bruce, 1966), *The Human Dimensions of Catechetics* (Bruce, 1967), *Growing in Grace* (Gastonia, 1968), *The Pearl and the Seed* (Allyn and Bacon, 1969), *Heschel: Religious Educator* (Dimensions, 1972), *The Gospel of the Holy Spirit* (Arena Lettres), and *The Kingdom and the Glory* (Arena Lettres, 1976). His articles have appeared in *America, Lamp, Worship, Momentum,* and the *Notre Dame Journal of Education.*

RANDOLPH CRUMP MILLER is Horace Bushnell Professor of Christian Nurture at the Divinity School of Yale University, and editor of *Religious Education.* An ordained priest of the Episcopal Church, Professor Miller received his bachelor's degree in philosophy from Pomona College and his doctorate in philosophy and religion from Yale University. He holds honorary doctorates from the Pacific School of Religion, the Church Divinity School of the Pacific, and the Episcopal Theological School. A specialist in religious education and theology, Dr. Miller has been the recipient of a fellowship from the American Association of Theological Schools, and another from the World Council of Christian Education. Prior to assuming his present academic post, Professor Miller served as instructor, assistant professor, associate professor, and professor at the Church Divinity School of the Pacific, and later as professor of Christian education on the Luther Weigle Fund at Yale University. Visiting professorships which Dr. Miller has held include ones at the Episcopal Theological School, Union Theological Seminary of New York, Syracuse University, Ecumenical Institute of the World Council of Churches (Switzerland), Garrett Theological Seminary, Berkeley Divinity School, Serampore College (India), Near East School of Theology (Lebanon), Trinity College (Singapore), Pacific School of Religion, Boston College, and the School of Theology at Claremont. His pertinent nonacademic experience includes being vicar and rector of St. Alban's Church (Cal.), chaplain to the Episcopalian students at the University of California in Berkeley, director of Christian education of St. Paul's Church (Conn.) and later at Trinity Church (Conn.), member of the curriculum committee of the Division of Christian Education of the Episcopalian Church, and Chairman of the Board of the Religious Education Association. Professor Miller is a member of the Religious Education Association, and the Association of Professors and Researchers in Religious Education; he has held various executive posts in both groups. He is listed in *Who's Who in America*. Books which Randolph Crump Miller has written or edited include *What We Can Believe* (Scribner's, 1941), *A Guide for Church School Teachers* (Cloister, 1943), *Christianity and the Contemporary Scene* (Morehouse, 1943), *The Church and Organized Movements* (Harper, 1946), *Religion Makes Sense* (Seabury, 1950), *The Clue to Christian Education* (Scribner, 1950), *A Symphony of the Christian Year* (Seabury, 1954), *Education for Christian Living* (Prentice-Hall, 1956, 1963), *Biblical Theology and Christian Education* (Scribner, 1956), *Be Not Anxious* (Seabury, 1957), *I Remember Jesus* (Seabury, 1958), *What Is the Nature of Man?* (United Church Press, 1959), *Christian Nurture and the Church* (Scribner, 1961), *Your*

Child's Religion (Doubleday, 1962), *Youth Considers Parents as People* (Nelson, 1965), *The Language Gap and God* (Pilgrim, 1970), *Living with Anxiety* (Pilgrim, 1971), *Live until You Die* (Pilgrim, 1973), *The American Spirit in Theology* (Pilgrim, 1974), and *This We Can Believe* (Hawthorn, 1976). His articles have appeared in the *Journal of Religion, Anglican Theological Review, Christian Century, Religion in Life,* and *Religious Education.*

CARL F. H. HENRY is lecturer-at-large of World Vision International and editor-at-large of *Christianity Today.* An ordained minister of the American Baptist Church, the Reverend Henry received a bachelor's degree in philosophy from Wheaton College, a bachelor's degree in divinity from the Northern Baptist Theological Seminary, a master's degree in theology from Wheaton College, a doctor's degree in the philosophy of religion from the Northern Baptist Theological Seminary, and a doctor's degree in philosophy from Boston University. He was awarded the honorary doctorate from Houghton College and from Wheaton College. A specialist in theology, Dr. Henry was the recipient of the Religious Heritage in America award, business and professional category, for contributions to the field of education. As Professor Henry, he has taught at the Northern Baptist Seminary and at Fuller Theological Seminary, and served as visiting professor at Eastern Baptist Seminary. He was the editor-in-chief of *Christianity Today* for thirteen years. The Reverend Henry is listed in *Who's Who in the World, Who's Who in America, Who's Who in Religion, Dictionary of International Biography,* and *Men of Achievement.* He holds membership in the American Theological Society, the American Philosophical Association, the Evangelical Theological Society, the American Society of Christian Ethics, and the Society for the Scientific Study of Religion. He is a former president of the Evangelical Theological Society, a former president of the Institute for Advanced Christian Studies, and a former vice-president of the American

Theological Society. Books which Dr. Henry has authored or edited include *The Pacific Garden Mission* (Zondervan, 1941, 147 pp.), *Successful Church Publicity* (Zondervan, 1942, 232 pp.), *The Uneasy Conscience of Modern Fundamentalism* (Eerdmans, 1947, 89 pp.), *Remaking the Modern Mind* (Eerdmans, 1948, 320 pp.), *Giving a Reason for Our Hope* (Wilde, 1949, 96 pp.), *The Protestant Dilemma* (Eerdmans, 1949, 248 pp.), *Notes on the Doctrine of God* (Wilde, 1950, 113 pp.), *Fifty Years of Protestant Theology* (Wilde, 1950, 113 pp.), *The Drift of Western Thought* (Eerdmans, 1951, 164 pp.), *Personal Idealism and Strong's Theology* (VanKampen, 1951, 233 pp.), *Glimpses of a Sacred Land* (Wilde, 1953, 240 pp.), *Christian Personal Ethics* (Eerdmans, 1957, 615 pp.), *Evangelical Responsibility in Contemporary Theology* (Eerdmans, 1957, 89 pp.), *Contemporary Evangelical Thought* (Harper, 1957, 320 pp.), *Revelation and the Bible* (Baker, 1959, 413 pp.), *The Biblical Expositor* (Holman, 1960, 1282 pp.), *Basic Christian Doctrines* (Holt, Rinehart and Winston, 1962, 302 pp.), *Christian Faith and Modern Theology* (Channel, 1964, 426 pp.), *Aspects of Christian Social Ethics* (Eerdmans, 1964, 190 pp.), *Frontiers in Modern Theology* (Moody Press, 1966, 160 pp., translated into Portuguese and into Norwegian), *The God Who Shows Himself* (Word, 1966, 138 pp.), *Jesus of Nazareth: Saviour and Lord* (Eerdmans, 1966, 277 pp.), *Evangelicals at the Brink of Crisis* (Word, 1967, 120 pp.), *Faith at the Frontiers* (Moody Press, 1969, 204 pp.), *A Plea for Evangelical Demonstration* (Baker, 1969, 124 pp.), *New Strides of Faith* (Moody Press, 1972, 140 pp.), *Fundamentals of the Faith* (Zondervan, 1973, 291 pp.), *Baker's Dictionary of Christian Ethics* (Baker, 1973, 726 pp.), *Evangelicals in Search of Identity* (Word, 1976), and *God, Revelation and Authority,* 2 volumes (Word, 1976). Dr. Henry's articles have appeared in *Theology Today, Commonweal, Interpretation, Review and Expositor,* and *Christianity Today.*

JOHN H. WESTERHOFF III is associate professor of religion and education at the Divinity School of Duke University. An ordained minister of the United Church of Christ, the Reverend Westerhoff received his bachelor's degree in psychology from Ursinus College, his master's degree in divinity from Harvard University, and his doctorate in education from Columbia University. A specialist in religious education, Professor Westerhoff is a consultant to the National Foundation for the Improvement of Education. He has been a visiting lecturer at Union Theological Seminary in New York, at Princeton Theological Seminary, and at Andover Newton Theological Seminary. Dr. Westerhoff served as Lentz Lecturer at the Divinity School of Harvard University, and as Adjunct Associate Professor at Fordham University. As the Reverend Westerhoff, he pastored the Presque Isle Congregational Church (Maine) and the First Congregational Church (Massachusetts). He was minister of education at the Needham Congregational Church (Massachusetts), and the secretary for education of the United Church Board for Homeland Ministries. Dr. Westerhoff was the editor of *Colloquy*. He is listed in *Who's Who in Religion, Who's Who in Education, Who's Who in the South,* and the *International Dictionary of Biography*. Professor Westerhoff holds membership in the Religious Education Association, the Association of Professors and Researchers in Religious Education, the Society for the Scientific Study of Religion, the National Education Association, and the American Anthropological Association. He is on the editorial board of the Religious Education Association, of the *Journal of Current Issues,* and of *New Conversations*. Books authored or edited by Dr. Westerhoff include *Values for Tomorrow's Children* (Pilgrim, 1970), *A Colloquy on Christian Education* (Pilgrim, 1972), *Liberation Letters* (United Church Press, 1973), *Learning to be Free* (United Church Press, 1973), *Generation to Generation* (Pilgrim, 1974), *Tomorrow's Church* (Word, 1976), *Will Our Children Have Faith?* (Seabury, 1976), and *W. H. McGuffey and His Readers* (Abingdon, 1976). Articles by Professor Westerhoff have appeared in *Religious Education, Christian Century, Catechist, Colloquy,* and *Duke Review*.

GLORIA DURKA is assistant professor and academic director in the Institute for the Study of Religion and Service at Boston College. A specialist in religious education, Professor Durka received her bachelor's degree in English from Medaille College, her master's degree in religious education from Fordham University, and her doctor's degree in religious education from New York University. She has served as an elementary school teacher and a high school teacher in Buffalo, instructor in the adult education program at Villa Maria College, instructor in the Harlem Tutorial Project at Emmaus House (New York City), instructor at Stonehill College, and lecturer in the Archdiocese of Portland's teacher-training institute. Dr. Durka also was a consultant to the seminar service of Sadlier. She is a member of the Religious Education Association, the Association of Professors and Researchers in Religious Education, Pi Lambda Theta, the American Academy of Religion, and the Association of Directors of Graduate Religious Education Programs. Professor Durka has held executive positions in the Association of Professors and Researchers in Religious Education and in the Association of Directors of Graduate Programs in Religious Education, as well as having served on the editorial board of *The Living Light*. Books authored or edited by Professor Durka include *Sexuality: Guidelines for a Four-Year High School Catechesis* (Fordham University Press, 1968), *Media, Morality, and Youth: A Teacher-Training Kit* (Sadlier, 1972), *Basic Guidelines for Creative Religious Education* (National Catholic Reporter cassette series, 1975), *Modeling God: Religious Education for Tomorrow* (Paulist, 1976), and *Emerging Issues in Religious Education* (Paulist, 1976). Her articles have appeared in *Religious Education, The Living Light, The Review of Books and Religion,* and *Aitia*.

JAMES MICHAEL LEE is professor of religious education at the University of Notre Dame. A specialist in religious education, Professor Lee received his bachelor's degree in philosophy and psychology from St. John's University (New York), his master's degree in history from Columbia University, and his doctor's degree in education from Columbia University. He has taught in the New York City public school system at the secondary level as well as in the adult education program. Professor Lee has also been lecturer in education at Seton Hall University, lecturer in education in the Graduate School of Hunter College, assistant professor of education at St. Joseph College (Conn.), and served as chairman of the Department of Graduate Studies in Education at the University of Notre Dame. He has been a Senior Fulbright Research Fellow at the University of Munich, and was the recipient of the Lilly Research and Training Fellowship of the Religious Education Association. Dr. Lee has served as an evaluator of a federally-funded education program for disadvantaged children and youth, a project consultant for the United States Office of Education, a special consultant for a national research project on Roman Catholic seminaries, and currently is a member of the Board of Lay Consultants, Education Section, of the National Conference of Catholic Men. He is listed in *Who's Who in the World*, *Who's Who in America*, *Who's Who in Religion*, *Catholic Who's Who*, *Dictionary of International Biography*, and *Contemporary Authors*. He holds memberships in the Religious Education Association, the Association of Professors and Researchers in Religious Education, the American Educational Research Association, the National Education Association, and the Society for the Scientific Study of Religion. Books authored or edited by Professor Lee include *Principles and Methods of Secondary Education* (McGraw-Hill, 1963, 619 pp.), *Seminary Education in a Time of Change* (Fides, 1965, 590 pp.), *Guidance and Counseling in Schools: Foundations and Processes* (McGraw-Hill, 1966, 612 pp.), *Readings in Guidance and Counseling* (Sheed and Ward, 1966), *Catholic Education in the Western World* (University of Notre Dame Press, 1967, 324 pp.), *The Purpose of Catholic Schooling* (National Catholic Educational Association and Pflaum, 1968, 80 pp.), *Toward a Future for Religious Education* (Pflaum, 1970, 252 pp.), *The Shape of Religious Education* (Religious Education Press, 1971, 330 pp.), *The Flow of Religious*

Education (Religious Education Press, 1973, 379 pp.), and *Forward Together: A Training Program for Religious Educators* (Thomas More Association, 1974, meditape program, 212 pages, 6 tapes). Articles by Professor Lee have appeared in *Religious Education, The Living Light, Catholic Educational Review, Theological Education,* and *Herder Correspondence.*

Index of Names

Index of Subjects